SMASHING THE

GLASS CEILING

Breaking Through Your
Personal Barriers
to Success

Bhupinder Anand

i

© Advisor Master Class 2013
10 Glentworth Street
London
NW1 5PG
UK
Tel: +44 207 486 5486
Fax: +44 207 486 5487
email: enquiries@advisormasterclass.com
web: www.advisormasterclass.com
ISBN: 978-0-9575607-0-3

To laugh often and love much; to win the respect of intelligent persons and the affection of children; to earn the approbation of honest citizens and endure the betrayal of false friends; to appreciate beauty; to find the best in others; to give of one's self; to leave the world a bit better, whether by a healthy child, a garden patch or a redeemed social condition; to have played and laughed with enthusiasm and sung with exultation; to know even one life has breathed easier because you have lived—this is to have succeeded."

Bessie Anderson Stanley

To Chris,

Think Big
+
Aim High!

Bhupinder

Dedication

My family has been very patient in both my career and during the writing of this book and I could not have done this, nor any of my other indulgences such as travelling the world to speak at conferences, without the support of my gorgeous wife, Daisy and my beautiful kids, Anishka and Savraj.

I also have a wonderful team behind me at Anand Associates upon whom I rely to keep my business going in my absence and they are like a second family to me.

I'm eternally grateful to my parents for giving me a valued family values system that still forms a hand of guidance in the decisions I make on daily basis. And to my brother and sister for their love, support and counselling.

Thank you.

Acknowledgements

As you go through this book, you will notice various characters and people who have been influential in my career. Some of these have been profound and others a little more subtle.

Some of these did not even know how they were helping me and, in some cases, neither did I at the time. The benefit of hindsight is a wonderful thing and when I look back at certain events in my life, I realise that small, even unremarkable actions have been very significant and noteworthy.

So, whilst it's impossible for me to name all of these people (some of you are mentioned in the text) I'd like to acknowledge anyone who has played a part in my life and my career and thank you for your support.

A special thanks must go to my good friends, John Shorter and Dil Patel, for their invaluable support, help and guidance in proofing and editing this book.

About the Author

> *"Always be a first-rate version of yourself, instead of a second-rate version of somebody else."*
>
> *Judy Garland*

Bhupinder Anand is Managing Director of 'Anand Associates Ltd', a firm of Independent Financial Advisors based in Central London, England.

Following five years as a broker consultant with Scottish Equitable, Bhupinder was awarded Planned Savings 'IFA of the Year 1995' after just 14 months as an IFA. He has since been runner-up for the same title in 2000 and 2002

He again received the award in 2003 (from Financial Advisor newspaper), becoming the only IFA in the UK to win the award twice.

In 2007, a colleague at Anand Associates won the same award.

His firm, Anand Associates, has also been rated as the 'Best IFA in the Capital' by Evening Standard newspaper.

His business has been profiled many times by various publications as a model practice for the benefit of other financial advisors.

He was the first personal finance editor for Eastern Eye, an English language newspaper with a circulation of 40,000 per week, and has been commissioned to write features and articles for many other publications. He has also had his own TV series on satellite, and is a regular guest on various radio and TV stations.

Bhupinder is a regular columnist in 'Money Marketing' newspaper expressing his views and opinions on the state of the UK Financial Services Industry.

In 1998, Anand Associates sponsored the 'Britain's Richest Asian 200' magazine, and Bhupinder shared the platform at the launch event with UK Prime Minister, Tony Blair.

He is qualified to Advanced Financial Planning Certificate level and is an Associate of the Chartered Insurance Institute.

Bhupinder is a 17-year member (as at 2013) of the Million Dollar Round Table MDRT[1], with 13 years as a Top of the Table (TOT).

Bhupinder has spoken at regional meetings of the UK's Life Insurance Association, Society of Financial Advisors and Personal Finance Society

---

[1] MDRT is also known as the Association of Professional Advisors and represent the world's top 40,000 financial advisors.

and at their Annual Conferences and delivered a keynote address at the Bank of England.

Bhupinder is acknowledged as one of the finest global speakers, particularly in the financial services profession. He is sought after as a keynote speaker for major conferences and travels extensively.

He has given presentations at many overseas conventions, including in Ireland, Poland, India, Egypt, Thailand, Malaysia, Singapore, Mexico, Australia, Philippines,

Bhupinder Anand
Addressing 7,500 delegates on the
Main Platform of the
MDRT Annual Meeting in
Anaheim, California, June 2004

Taiwan, Japan, Slovakia, Lithuania, Cyprus, Greece, Turkey, Canada and the USA.

He is a popular speaker at MDRT conferences and has spoken at MDRT meetings in San Francisco, Nashville, Los Angeles, Naples, Palm Springs, Denver, New Orleans, Atlanta, Tokyo and Hyderabad, India plus the honour of addressing 7,500 delegates on the MDRT Main Platform, see www.tinyurl.com/cmckhzo.

At the 2007 MDRT Annual Meeting in Denver, he was the highest rated presenter out of 58 focus session speakers.

He has spoken four years in a row at the Critical Illness Insurance Conference and in 2009 was a keynote speaker at the APLIC Congress in Macau, China.

He has also three times given a keynote address on business and life planning as an alumni of his old university, Oxford Brookes.

Bhupinder is a passionate believer in the value of Independent Financial Advice, and the need for holistic financial planning to help people to achieve their goals and objectives in life.

Through his desire to help grow his chosen profession and to increase advisor skills and expertise, Bhupinder has launched his Advisor Master Class training program to rave reviews and influenced the success of many financial advisers around the world.

If you would like to book Bhupinder as a speaker for your conference, please contact him on +44 207 486 5486 or Bhupinder@advisormasterclass.com.

Contents

1/ Introduction

> *"Twenty years from now you will be more disappointed by the things that you didn't do than by the ones you did. So throw off the bowlines. Catch the trade winds in your sails. Explore. Dream. Discover."*
>
> Mark Twain

I've always wanted to be a financial advisor.

Well, that's not quite true. Apparently (according to my mother), when I was much younger (and too far back for me to remember now), I wanted to be a milkman. Seemingly, the thought of travelling the highways in my electric milk float, dropping off bottles of cream-top and collecting the empties, was my dream career.

Maybe I was able to foresee that this unique career was not one that was going to last, as it was, fortunately, not one that I pursued proactively. The noble art of milk bottle delivery has now pretty much dried out; in hindsight, sadly, I lacked the foresight to invent disposable milk cartons instead!

I've tried to reconcile this original career desire with where I am now and find that there are some intriguing parallels. Maybe the simple thought of being on the open roads, enjoying the fresh air, meeting different people and having interesting conversations was a catalyst of thought in my junior head. Perhaps the feeling of freedom and independence were what attracted me. Possibly the notion that I was doing a valuable service for others and that, without me, how miserable their lives would be, families deprived of milk on their breakfast table.

In the end, despite these commendable ambitions, I think it was the distressing chore of having to do desperately early mornings that must have changed my mind!

What I have come to realise over the course of many years since then is that I have actually made some pretty profound decisions that have affected who I am today. Some of those decisions were conscious and considered, whilst many were very much unconscious and only retrospectively recognisable with the passage of time.

Of course, we all make profound decisions in one way or another, and I certainly don't consider myself as anyone special. Yet, what I have gradually realised is that I am one of those people who relish the challenge of a challenge. I look at life as a series of obstacles to be overcome and, rather than taking the easy route, I will quite often explore an alternative strategy. One that may be more difficult, one that may be less obvious, one that others would shy away from, but one that I feel makes me stronger as an individual.

As such, whenever I have found myself facing what for many people would be a barrier or 'Glass Ceiling' or reason to give up, I choose to confront it head-on. I will define what a 'Glass Ceiling' is shortly.

In this book, I want to share some of my life experiences in order to help others understand how they too could challenge some of their own Glass Ceilings, tackle some of their own pre-conceptions and realise their own full potential.

Having said that, I must emphasise what this book is *not*. I do not claim for it to be an academic work or a piece of major intellectual research. I do not profess to be sharing any revolutionary new secret techniques.

What I will be doing, however, is giving my take on things that I have learned and how I have interpreted them and used them. I have distilled numerous ideas and concepts and connected them to my own experiences in order to help you appreciate how you can achieve the success you deserve.

This book came about because of the feedback I have had from speeches that I have given over the years and demand for more from delegates.

Some of the content of this book has been used in speeches given at conferences all around the world and the results have been truly dramatic, with some delegates having a sudden moment of self-realisation that success was theirs to grasp and that all it took was a change of mind-set. I have been honoured to have received countless feedback from people who have said that their lives have been changed because they applied the ideas and tools that were being shared with them.

With the application of some of the principles and concepts in this book, I hope that you too will find some practical strategies that will make an insightful change in your life.

As you open each chapter, you will note that I have provided a quotation that I feel is relevant to that specific chapter. They have not been chosen randomly, and each one has been carefully selected to reflect the content of that section. I would ask that, before you commence each chapter, please read the quotation and consider what those words mean to you personally. After reading the chapter, then please do re-visit the quote and re-consider what the quote means to you now based upon what you may have learned.

As you read this book, you may find that some of the ideas and concepts are fairly simple and straight-forward. I don't disagree. The reality is, though, that many people don't actually take enough time to sit back and think about the issues and the strategies that need to be implemented.

If this book helps to remind you of some of the things that you know you should do but never seem to get around to doing, then it is doing its job.

2/ Defining a "Glass Ceiling"

> *"To live is the rarest thing in the world. Most people exist, that is all."*
>
> Oscar Wilde

Traditionally, and quite appropriately, the term "Glass Ceiling" has typically implied a sense of institutional injustice. It has been commonly understood to be a form of discrimination against a minority group by a large corporation or body, which limits the ability of an individual to achieve their desires and ambitions, irrespective of their innate ability to do so.

It usually takes the form of one of the 'isms' – typically, racism, sexism, ageism and disability discrimination. To some extent, it may also include the concept of the 'old-boy' network, whereby if you didn't attend the 'right' college or university, your career path would inevitably be restricted, preference being given to members of that clique. You knew you deserved better, but the world seemed to be conspiring against you and there was very little that you could do about it.

The concept of the Glass Ceiling is that the individual can see where their skills and expertise should take them in their career path, but there are unwritten rules, undiscussed barriers, unpublicised impediments to their progress. The prevailing attitude by your superiors is that you just don't fit the mould, you should not be thinking above your station, you should just accept it and be happy with where you are, be grateful that at least you have a job.

To a very large extent, with anti-discrimination legislation and a more understanding culture that people should be judged purely on their merits and not on their race, sex, religion or any other abstract criteria, the phrase of suffering from the effect of a Glass Ceiling is much less common than it used to be.

For the purposes of the definition I am going to use throughout this book, I have chosen the term 'Glass Ceiling' to have a specific, modernised, definition. That is:

You have a clear vision of what you want in your future (short, medium or long-term) but there is something in the way that obscures that mental picture. You can see what you want, but there seems to be a transparent barrier or series of obstacles to achieving your dreams.

Take a moment to study that statement and think about what it means to you right now in your personal and professional life.

Clearly, people are able to have more than one

Glass Ceiling in different ways and can have different Glass Ceilings affecting different aspects of their lives.

Can you empathise with the above definition in some way?

You are frustrated with the way things are going and you feel that your talent is being wasted.

You know you have the potential to succeed...if only you were given the chance to do so.

You relish the opportunity of flying with the winners, but there seems to be a limitation on your ability to do so.

You see others achieving success but wonder why it seems to somehow elude you.

You feel like you are looking at the top of a skyscraper where your dreams lie awaiting you.

But, as you try to reach out to touch them, and even though you know you can, your ability to grasp that bundle of aspirations is impeded by a thick, laminated window that continually frustrates you.

Why is it that others around you don't seem to have these problems? Do they have some special abilities that you simply don't possess or have access to? What would happen if you could get a taste of this magic potion, just occasionally? How would your life change?

Do you *really* think that others have acquired some kind of magic potion, some form of magic elixir that gives them extraordinary supernatural powers? Do they have some special gift that God gave them and cruelly denied you?

No, of course not!

Or are they ... just perhaps ... however remotely possible ... just maybe ... doing things that you are not?

And what would happen if you could learn a few of these techniques? Would you Smash through your Glass Ceiling to leap to the top of the skyscraper? Are you even willing to try?

Do you have the courage to do what it takes?

Indeed, do you truly have the *desire* to do what it takes?

So many questions!

But just imagine the possibilities if you could shatter this transparent barricade...

In fact, before you move on to the next chapter, I'd like you to pause for a few moments to consider what life is going to look like for you, say, ten years from today; I want you to stretch your thoughts and ambitions, but if ten years still seems too far, then work on five years for now.

In doing this exercise, as I have previously stated, do not necessarily confine yourself to material things. Additionally, and more importantly, think about your goals in terms of what kind of person you want to become. What is your role going to be with your family, your career, your clients, your team, society and community? How will you be a role model in each of these aspects?

Think of it this way; in ten years' time from today, what opinion do you want people to have about you? What will they think about you and what will they be saying about you? It is not egotistical, but it is important to each of us in our lives that our peers have a good opinion of us, it helps us to define our goals and objectives in the context of the person we want to be.

Of course, it doesn't necessarily mean that people have a bad opinion of us now that needs to be changed. It's about maintaining and enhancing the good reputation we have.

Allow your dreams to shape your future, and then we can move on to tackling the obstacles that are going to come your way, the Glass Ceilings that need to be Smashed.

A Side-note on the Meaning of 'Desire'

Desire is such a powerful emotion, it is binary in nature; you either have it or you don't. Desire is not measured on a scale of one to ten, it is absolute.

Desire is what makes you take the action you need to in order to move forward positively.

Yet, in the English language, we have a very strange phrase, when we say that someone has "half-hearted desires". Just what does that mean!!

On the grounds that desire is something you either have or you don't, half-hearted desires are the same as having no desire at all.

Indeed, I would even go further to say that, if something else will suffice as a second choice or there is an alternative to your desire, the main thing was never a desire, it was just a preference.

I will use the word 'desire' again later in the book and so it is important to understand and appreciate my clear definition of the meaning and value of that word.

In the next chapter, I'll help you recognise your personal current Glass Ceiling, before moving on to strategies that you can use to liberate yourself from the shackles of these constraints.

3/ Identifying Your Own Glass Ceilings

> *"Do not go where the path may lead, go instead where there is no path and leave a trail."*
>
> *Ralph Waldo Emerson*

Some people have a clear and vivid vision of what life will look like for them ten years from now. Others will struggle to say what life looks like ten days from now and are even scared to think of any longer timescale!

This book is not about creating your vision or setting goals (I have a separate forthcoming book for that[2]) and many other authors can help you in crafting yours. This book is about addressing the barriers to achieving that vision. Having said that, in a later chapter, I will explore some of the principles involved in setting a vision and the power and benefit of doing so.

Whatever our goals are, each of us has a Glass Ceiling through which we see view these aspirations. We have a feeling that our vision cannot become a

---

[2] An additional book to this will be called 'Be the Person you Want to be in 10 Years' Time, Today'

reality as we cannot break through this Glass Ceiling that suppresses our growth.

We know what we want ... we just can't seem to get there.

In order to destroy these Glass Ceilings, it would, of course, be very useful to know what those Glass Ceilings are in the first place. (Note, I use the plural of Glass Ceiling as I do believe that people have different Glass Ceilings that affect different parts of their lives. Some of these may be common to several areas and, often, fixing one has a domino effect on others).

I'd like you to do the following exercise. In fact, to get the very best out of your investment in this book, it's important that you *actually* do this. You will get a huge amount more out of it if you do the exercise rather than imagine it.

Take a clean sheet of paper and put the heading **'My Vision'** at the top of it.

In the previous chapter, I asked you to just think about this vision. Now, I want you to be more specific. Take a few minutes (about 15 to 20 should be plenty, but take as long you feel you need) and list out your future dreams and desires, your aspirations and ambitions, your goals and objectives. You should place some time frame on them or just group them as short, medium or long-term goals. Short, medium and long should in turn have some time definitions, perhaps one, five and ten years.

It is important to be as thorough and detailed as possible in compiling this list. The more work you put into it now, the better the planning is going to be and the better the impact on the result. The more detailed you can be, the better. This list will form the view of the top of the skyscraper, with the blue sky of freedom that will come from achieving these goals sitting beyond that.

They should not be just material things but also include things that will define how you will feel in achieving those goals.

How will they motivate you, inspire you and satisfy you?

What sense of freedom, liberation and independence will they provide?

How will they be significant to you, your family, your friends, your team, your clients, your colleagues and peers, your community and others?

While being realistic and achievable with effort, your vision should, nevertheless, be challenging.

Many people use the phrase when setting their goals, 'if you don't know where you are heading, how will you know when you get there?'

A Side-note on Creating Your Vision

Your vision document is a vital part of the process in Smashing your Glass Ceiling. However, you will only be compelled to take the relevant action if you have bought into the Vision emotionally.

Whatever you wrote down, I'd like you to ask yourself two additional questions against each point.

Firstly, 'Why is that important to me?' If you don't think it is important or struggle to attach importance to it, then it isn't really part of your Vision. It's a half-hearted Desire, which we have already established is worthless, the same as having no Desire. It might be something you want, but if it isn't important enough to you, you won't care to do something about it.

After answering the first question, whatever your answer is, ask yourself the following question about that answer, 'And, what's important about that to me?'

This second question will distil your item to an emotional response, even if what you started with was a material item.

Do this now, before you move on. Get the right emotional attachment to your decisions and you become a powerful, unstoppable individual.

Specifically, 'if you don't have a sense of direction about your future, how will you know what decisions to make when you have choices that will confront you?'

In a similar vein, but often less considered is, 'if you don't know what the barriers are, how will you devise a strategy to destroy them?'

Or, if you fail to have the honesty and discipline to recognise your personal Glass Ceilings, you will always be left wondering why success eludes you.

Clearly then, being honest and transparent with yourself about what you believe are your personal Glass Ceilings is key to challenging them. No-one is going to tell you what your Glass Ceilings are, although it's always interesting to ask someone what they think they are for you. Indeed, someone else's idea of what are your Glass Ceilings is often food for thought. Do take such answers as an opportunity to be reflective and learn from what is being said rather than taking it as an attack. Moments of self-realisation can often come from taking another's opinion.

However, for the purposes for this exercise, a Glass Ceiling is only one if you have taken personal ownership of it and are willing to recognise it as such.

Having stated your vision and goals, (and you can

always add to them later), now take another clean sheet of paper and put the heading **'My Glass Ceilings'** at the top of it.

Take a few minutes (again, around 15 should be plenty, but take as long as you need) and make a list of all the possible things that you feel are currently blocking your way to the success you dream of. This is a crucial and essential step to Smashing your Glass Ceilings.

Again, actually doing this exercise is considerably better than just thinking about it.

Some of the items on your list will be obvious and fairly common to many people (maybe money, state of the economy, regulation and compliance, family, team, lack of confidence, lack of focus, etc.), but some will be highly personal and unique to you. Treat this as a private moment of self-reflection. No-one is going to challenge you on the validity, accuracy or thoroughness of your list. You need to be emotionally involved with your Glass Ceilings, not merely a list of words. You should really feel strongly about what you have written.

Think beyond the obvious. Go deep inside and be honest with your answers. Analyse your flaws that you recognise. Consider what it is that you really don't like doing. Reflect on what it is that you are not good at but would like to be and need to be in order to achieve your goals.

This list is going to become your work in progress and so its accuracy and relevance is vital. The longer and more complete the list, the more work you will have to do, but the stronger and more successful you will become.

Do this now, before you move on the next section; the next step will make more sense to you if you put the effort in now.

Done?

Now, place this list in front of you and to the right hand side of it, place your vision document. Study these two documents carefully and visualise how, if the list of Glass Ceilings to the left did not exist, your visions could easily be achieved. It is these barriers that block your way and we need to remove them, we have to Smash these Glass Ceilings!

To do this, we are going to do something so incredibly simple, but also immensely insightful. Doing this next step will not yet Smash your Glass Ceilings, but will give you the hammer with which to take aim. In fact, over the course of the rest of this book, I am going to provide you with a complete tool kit with which to attack your Glass Ceilings, but let's start with the most important step.

This next step is so simple that you will initially wonder how it is going to make a difference, yet the results will be instinctively profound. Just reading it, it may seem so obvious, and you may initially question how it will make a difference, but by actively engaging with the exercise, you will maximise the benefit and experience the deep insight, which it provides.

Ready?

With the two pages side by side, simply change the heading on the list of Glass Ceilings from 'My Glass Ceilings' to **'My Opportunities'**.

Now look at the two sheets, side by side, again and visually re-connect the two.

Something quite significant should now occur to you. A simple, yet deep and thoughtful, moment of self-realisation.

Suddenly, your vision seems much more achievable. Just by changing the list of your barriers, your Glass Ceilings into a list of Opportunities, you should have a different perspective on the problem.

Yes, it is simple and is a variation of the classic phrase of whether you consider a glass filled halfway with water as being half-full or half-empty.

Beyond that, however, what was previously seen as

a list of obstacles must now be recognised as actually merely being a list of excuses. We haven't removed the Glass Ceilings, we've just altered our stance towards them, our view and our perspective of them. The list remains, but our opinion and feeling about it is different. Consider that instead of being blinded by the sunlight, we are using the same light to illuminate our direction.

We haven't yet Smashed the Glass Ceiling, but we have now realised that our attitude towards it is devastatingly different.

This may seem highly simplistic (and I admit that it is!) but what it does is to define our approach to our future success. Our attitude towards a problem is also the solution to the problem. In fact, perhaps it is our attitude that is the underlying problem and not the issue itself.

Think about that for a moment...perhaps it is our attitude that is the underlying problem and not the issue itself.

You see, if we think that our Glass Ceilings are a barrier to our success, then we focus upon them as obstructions. We get frustrated with all the reasons why these complications exist and we search for excuses. We blame others and we feel bitter about our failures rather than learning from them.

Sure, sometimes these Glass Ceilings are imposed

upon us by others, as I described earlier when an institution (overtly or covertly) uses the 'isms of racism, sexism, etc. to undeservedly hold people with talent back. I will later show how I have personally experienced and challenged some of these issues.

Additionally, of course, I do recognise that there will be personal circumstances and tragedies that, usually only temporarily, cause a pause in your continued success. It is up to you whether you define such events as Glass Ceiling or not.

One of the fundamental points to realise is that most of the Glass Ceilings we face are not real ... they actually exist only in our mind. Often self-created in our own minds and often self-perpetuating and self-justifying, we let these Glass Ceilings control our decisions and actions.

Instead of looking for excuses or blaming others or circumstances, many Glass Ceilings sit firmly between our two ears, lodged firmly in our brains as our mind-set. And the longer they have been there, the harder they are to dislodge.

By carrying out the exercise described earlier, what you will now have realised is that it is your own attitude that determines the effect or impact of a so-called Glass Ceiling. If you view it as an obstacle, guess what, it is!

And if you were to distance yourself from it as a Glass Ceiling and view it from an alternative perspective as an exciting opportunity, guess what, it is!

It is our mind-set that needs to be updated and upgraded and our self-belief or perhaps lack of self-belief) confronted.

The genuine challenge then is in understanding how to capture and take advantage of the opportunities that we listed. Truly successful people have firstly identified what the opportunities are, those that others perceive as stumbling blocks, and then used their creativity and ingenuity to tackle them.

Anyone can do this, if their attitude is directed with the right energies in the right direction.

Hopefully you, too, have now started to appreciate the common phrase: 'Whether you believe you can, or whether you believe you can't, either way, you're right'. You will achieve only what you believe you can achieve and, until you honestly believe that you can, then frustration will prevail.

Having set up these obstacles and converted them into opportunities, we need to consider how our attitude toward them can be manipulated further. We need to appreciate the important distinction between our Fear of Failure and our Desire for

Success.

Don't throw away your converted list of Glass Ceilings yet as we're going to return to this list later in the book.

4/ Fear of Failure vs. Desire for Success

> *"Everything you do is triggered by an emotion of either desire or fear."*
>
> *Brian Tracy*

Whether Glass Ceilings are imposed on us by others or by ourselves, we either believe that we can't break through these invisible barriers or, more commonly and honestly, we are too afraid to take on the risks to do so.

We focus more on the problem itself than we do on the benefits of fixing the problem. A little like some financial advisory clients, who use the 'problem' of lack of money now to avoid the future, much bigger, problem of leaving their family and themselves without sufficient funds to support their lifestyle.

The exercise in the previous section will now have started to get you thinking differently; that is a good start, but it is not quite enough.

Realisation and appreciation of the problem is a perfect first step in dealing with it and, as already explored, converting the problem from a Glass Ceiling to an Opportunity is no doubt enlightening, which is great further progress. But, that is still only an academic exercise if no further action is taken and we stopped there.

The issue that holds most people back from trying is simply a *Fear* of *Failure*. This fear can be crippling and I believe is the key difference between those who are highly successful and those who are only moderately so.

I can't believe that anyone deliberately chooses to live their life being just average; actually, by definition, many people are above this notional benchmark and many are below, even if they think they are not. By reading this book, I assume that you are not interested in being just average, let alone below the line.

So, what makes the difference between a winner and a potential winner? By the way, did you notice the nuance of that statement? I don't believe that there are winners and losers, just winners and potential winners. The latter are just people who have not yet worked out how to take advantage of their latent potential and just need some more time and the right focus.

The difference is in their attitude towards risk. Or putting it another way, winners have realised that the greatest risk in life is not taking any risks. They have realised that Smashing Glass Ceilings is a risky exercise – some of the shards of glass could cause you damage if you don't take good care in assessing the risk and don't have a plan in place. But they know that, with adequate preparation and the right tools, the glass can be shattered safely and, indeed, has to be shattered for them to progress.

Otherwise, most people live their lives in a comfort zone. They have reached where they have reached and to do any more will require new effort and the engagement of risk. They have Glass Ceilings in their life but have become comfortable with them. These potential winners have made a key decision, often not realising that this assessment has even been made. They have subconsciously decided that their Fear of Failure exceeds their Desire for Success.

Contemplate that insightful statement for a moment:

A comfort zone surrounds us when our Fear of Failure outweighs our Desire for Success.

If that is true, then so is the converse, that true and sustained success follows for those who have decided that their Desire for Success outweighs their Fear of Failure.

We all have the capacity and potential for success, it's just whether we want it enough to challenge ourselves and our limiting beliefs, whether we are prepared to do what it takes to Smash through our personal Glass Ceilings.

Zig Ziglar [3] stated that "One of life's greatest tragedies is unrealised potential".

So, what a tragedy that people will not confront their Glass Ceilings to fully exploit the potential that they were born with. Imagine the powerful difference you could make to your family, your friends, your team, your clients, your colleagues and peers, your community and, of course, to yourself if you could fully exploit all the potential you possess or could acquire.

And why would you not wish to do that?

For example, how would you like the following on your gravestone or being read out as part of your eulogy:

---

[3] Sadly, motivational guru, Zig Ziglar, died on 28th November, 2012, aged 86

I don't think that too many people would be too happy about the second part of this!

Perhaps the headstone on the below would be a better tribute and testament to your phenomenal lifetime achievements:

In researching and considering analogies to describe unrealised potential, I was drawn to examples of where unknown potential had actually been realised. Potential which others had not even perceived existed. In each case, it was clear that the exploitation of potential required courage, imagination and creativity.

0In the art world, I was struck by two particular examples, from Michelangelo and Leonardo da Vinci, respectively. In Michelangelo's case, he had a unique vision, almost x-ray vision, in order to see

43

what was inside a block of stone. When he sculpted the Statue of David he created a thing of beauty that has stood the test of time. People flock to the Accademia Gallery in Florence, Italy to witness his magnificent creation.

Were he alive today, I believe he would claim that all he did was to release the potential that already existed inside the block of marble. He would say that the Statue of David was always there, inside that block of dense stone, and the only part he played was to show the world what secrets the stone held. He liberated the incredible potential of the slab of marble.

Similarly, when he painted the Mona Lisa, Leonardo da Vinci would have said that it really was nothing more than oil paint on a sheet of canvas. At the time, its value was not much greater than that of the cost of the raw materials. It is the passage of time that created its value and fame.

In fact, I use the example of the Mona Lisa to describe what I do as a financial advisor when I sell life insurance. All that I do is arrange for a drop of ink on a piece of paper to be issued in the name of a client. At that particular time, its value is nothing more than the cost of the raw materials. But it's the promise to pay and the passage of time that will create a masterpiece, something of value and beauty to those who will ultimately benefit from it.

Leonardo da Vinci realised the potential of the raw materials and, in my own very small way, in understanding what I do for my clients, so do I.

A sculptor, by the name of Gutzon Borglum, was another man who could visualise potential. He viewed a mountain and saw something that it contained that no-one had previously seen. He had a vision for Mount Rushmore in South Dakota, USA.

Borglum saw that the mountain retained a huge secret and he considered it as his role in life to get the mountain to release its potential for the world to see.

Incredibly, his vision could see that inside the mountain were representations of four US President's heads, George Washington, Thomas Jefferson, Abraham Lincoln and Theodore Roosevelt and he had the courage to show the world what could be achieved.

Mount Rushmore, South Dakota , USA.
Each of the heads is 18 metres in height.

Borglum made it his life's mission to expose those amazing structures. He so demonstrably had absolutely no Fear of Failure.

Borglum would also argue that he didn't create the

heads, they were already there, it was simply his role to assist the mountain in realising its own potential.

Do you recognise a theme here that you could apply to your own life?

You have the potential inside of you to achieve amazing things in your life. No-one is going to give you *potential*, it's already there in your very being. All that authors and speakers such as myself and those far more experienced than me can do is to help you realise your own latent potential.

We can't provide you with potential. All that we can do is to share you with some tools that will help you recognise your own dreams and aspirations and then help you Smash the Glass Ceilings that prevent you from achieving your full and beautiful potential.

We can motivate and inspire you but, ultimately, it has to be *you* that instigates the necessary changes in your life.

The reality is that it is only when your genuine Desire for Success exceeds your Fear of Failure that you will make the required change. And this desire for success must be deep-rooted, not something you simply switch on and off depending upon your mood.

Have you noticed how truly successful people constantly carry a sense of energy and pride in who they are and what they stand for. You can sense it in how they talk, how they behave and how they interact with others. They exude confidence and charisma in the secure knowledge that they are constantly and fully exploiting their own potential and they seem to have a clear sense of direction and purpose in their life.

I recall hearing a speaker urge her audience to look in the mirror each morning and tell themselves that 'today was going to be a great day!' Nothing wrong with that per se, but it is not a strategy that creates any real depth of self-belief – for example, what happens if you forget to do it one morning? Does it mean that you are going to have a terrible day because you failed to declare that today was going to be memorable day? Of course not.

Looking in the mirror for self-affirmation is not a bad thing to do, but it is only a minor tool in the much bigger picture of what is actually going in your head. It is arguably only part of a more significant strategy that is based up on moving away from a Fear of Failure.

People who are driven to constantly achieve do not need daily self-affirmation. Their self-belief and confidence is so strong that it is normal for each day to be great, and that any mishaps are actually seen as opportunities for learning and development. This comes from having a clear and compelling sense of direction, motivated by a strategy that is based upon a Desire for Success and driven by a clarity of Vision.

5/ The Three 'C' Zones

> *"Nowhere on your birth certificate did it say life would be fair."*
>
> Trevor Jones

After a period of learning new ideas, concepts and techniques, most of us reach a position of a feeling of control whereby things are going fairly smoothly, many of the previous problems and issues have been eliminated and we are fairly happy and comfortable. Indeed, some of us may be very pleased and content in our current comfort zone. But, I put it to you that that is potentially a very dangerous position to be in.

You see, when we learn something new that we can apply in our personal and professional lives, we enter a new **'Confidence Zone'**. Our life becomes more interesting as we practice our new skills to enhance and perfect them. It's not always easy, but as long as we learn from our mistakes, we grow as individuals. We carry a sense of energy and urgency about us as we feel that we are using and exploiting our latent potential. It is exciting and exhilarating when we are in this place and we feel that we can achieve absolutely anything we set our mind upon. We relish the challenge and we think and behave pro-actively.

People around us are excited alongside us too as we demonstrate our new expertise and seek new avenues to share it. Our motivation and self-inspiration is high because we have gained a new sense of Confidence.

This is, of course, a great, enjoyable, position to be in. But then something quite strange and gradual happens. We stop learning, we stop changing and we feel that things are going so well that we don't need to gain new confidences, new expertise or skills. We feel that we don't have the time, the inclination or perhaps even the desire or energy to learn new competences. We steadily, and often indiscernibly, enter a **'Comfort Zone'**. This is a place where we know what we're good at, we're enjoying exploiting our newly developed skills and we think we have 'made it'. The efforts of gaining new confidences are far behind us and we are coasting on the glory of this past success.

Now, that's okay if the world simply stopped where it is and nothing new ever happened. If there were never any new products, new legislation, new technology or new competition, then it would be fine to stand still and milk the expertise we have. But, that's just never going to be the case.

The world is constantly changing and we have to constantly change and adapt with it. Perhaps it's our Fear of Failure that outweighs our Desire for

Success that is holding us back from reaching a new Confidence Zone.

And this Fear of Failure is quietly destructive. For, without the energising effect of creating a new Confidence Zone, our Comfort Zone will slowly but surely become a **'Complacency Zone'**. This is a very dangerous place to be.

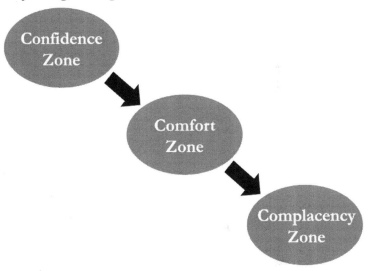

In the Complacency Zone, we simply don't notice or realise that we are not engaging with the constant change that is happening around us. We either don't realise it or, more commonly, perhaps even lazily, choose to ignore it. We believe it won't affect us as we are comfortable where we are.

Even when change is notified to us and we know it is on its way, those in the Complacency Zone will refuse to acknowledge its existence.

A good example of this is the massive changes that have been inflicted upon the UK financial services profession with effect from January 2013 by the Financial Services Authority, through the regulator's Retail Distribution Review (RDR). This dramatic and wholesale change was indicated many years before, through several consultative documents and processes and plenty of notice given of subsequent forthcoming change. Primarily, it introduced two major and potentially game-changing upheavals – the introduction of higher levels of minimum qualifications and the abolition of commissions on investment products, forcing financial advisors to discuss their fees and income transparently with their clients.

I make no comment or judgement as to whether these are positive or negative developments, although, I must admit that my own business was ready for these changes ten years before they were even dreamed up by the regulator, perhaps a good indication of someone who lives in a Confidence Zone, seeking out new opportunities that others are not even considering.

But, I do pass observation on the attitude of financial advisors to this change, depending upon which of the three Zones they were in as the changes were announced.

Those who were already in a Confidence Zone, who had robust business models and had already become confident with charging fees and being transparent about how they added value to the client relationship were not disturbed by these changes. They had reached more than the new minimum qualifications already and embraced the change.

Those who were in the Comfort Zone had to make a decision. They had to instigate change, either to gain the new qualifications and learn new techniques to demonstrate that they added value to the client relationship or work out how they were going to sell their businesses in the foreseeable future. Either way was uncomfortable, because change had sneaked up on them, even though it had announced its forthcoming arrival with plenty of notice. Time had simply passed quicker than any of this group had realised and now they were being forced to make difficult assessments on their business model.

Having said that, time was something which those in the Complacent Zone had no concept of. They refused to acknowledge that change would actually happen, believing that it was too radical and that it would be rescinded. They either made no changes, living in the forlorn hope that the regulator would, somehow, change its mind. Instead of instigating change, they fought it, even engaging politicians to take up the cause. Again, I make no comments on the merits of the new regulations or otherwise, but they were terrified of what was going to happen as they had simply left it too late to practice and perfect their new model.

I had written articles in the trade press about the need to make the changes, which would take say three months, then adapt to those changes for another, say three months, practice the new way of working, make the mistakes and learn from them, which would take a further three months to convert and then be ready for at least six months before the new regulations came into force. That means being ready almost two years before the date of implementation, yet, with one year to go, more than half of UK financial advisors were still running their business the way they always had.

I can only surmise that such advisers were certainly not in a Confidence Zone, were more probably in a Comfort Zone, imagining that any changes would not affect them and those in the Complacency Zone had such a long way to change that they were pretty much giving in.

In the first quarter of 2013, there were estimates that around 20% of all UK financial advisers had left the profession, which is a damning statistic. Perhaps against those that just gave up and, even though I have sought not to make comment in this book, (I do condemn the regulator in my newspaper articles) against a narrow-sighted regulator that failed to appreciate the real world effect of their bureaucratic ideas.

I recall a speech I gave at a UK conference on how to change and adapt to charging fees. In the debrief discussion that followed, one delegate was heard to say 'that simply doesn't happen in the real world', as if what I had been saying was a complete fabrication. Fortunately, a colleague from my company who was sitting at the same table was able to verify my comments, but it struck me that here was someone who was so firmly entrenched in a Complacency Zone that he could not even see that others were able to operate a different model to his.

I'll share a little more about handling change and coping with change in a later chapter.

At this stage, you should give honest and careful consideration of which of the three zones you think you are currently in, both in personal aspects of your life and professional. If in the latter two zones, the next question will be what you are going to do about it to exploit the potential you have?

Being in a Confidence Zone is obviously the ideal situation, although regularly addressing this question will establish if you are sliding out of this.

Depending upon whether you are currently in a Comfort Zone or a Complacency Zone will determine the strategy you need to employ to move back up to the Confidence Zone.

In the Comfort Zone, moving back to the Confidence Zone is about continually adapting the skills you already have, perhaps thinking about applying them to a new marketing strategy or positioning exercise, or how to use them in a different way; the classic 'thinking out of the box'. I call this your 'Tactical Planning' and it is about keeping ahead of change as it occurs.

In the Complacency Zone, a more fundamental strategy is required rather than subtle changes. Having allowed yourself slide to this zone, you need to have a complete re-appraisal of what you are currently doing. Significant change has occurred and now you need to do something significant to catch up.

This could involve learning new skills and expertise and even re-considering what you are offering and who you are offering it to. Dramatic change is required to make a positive effect.

In the context of the person you want to be in the future, you need to know where your starting position is now, so it is good to recognise which 'C' Zone you currently occupy in relationship to differ-

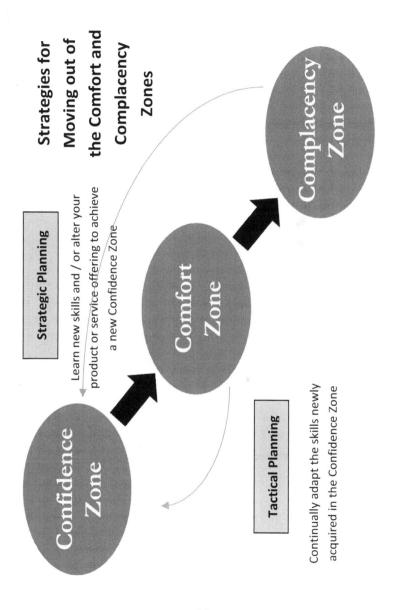

Strategies for Moving out of the Comfort and Complacency Zones

Strategic Planning

Learn new skills and / or alter your product or service offering to achieve a new Confidence Zone

Complacency Zone

Comfort Zone

Confidence Zone

Tactical Planning

Continually adapt the skills newly acquired in the Confidence Zone

ent aspects of your ambitions. Only then can you employ the appropriate strategy to move you forward.

Tactical Planning

In the Comfort Zone, you have learned some new skills and techniques that you acquired that gave you sense of Confidence. Perhaps they were things you heard at a conference or seminar which made you think that this was an idea that you could use...but you never really applied it.

I have spoken at so many conferences where I have met an audience member some time later who recalls the speech I gave as having had an impact. But when challenged as to what they did after the conference, the answer is so often nothing at all. I wonder how many people do this after a training meeting? Of course, not you!

Perhaps it's time to revisit your notes and take another look at what caught your attention at the time, but you didn't implement. Obviously, that idea has worked for someone...could it work for you if you tried it?

Another observation is when people have used something new and it worked for them so they incorporated it into their daily activity. But gradually, over time, that habit seemed to die away and has been forgotten. Have a think about some ideas or strategies that worked for you but you have, without realising it, stopped doing. If they worked before, would they work now?

Make a list of the kind of things you used to do, perhaps a sales idea or marketing technique that worked and whether now is the time to consider re-using that. You will be surprised at what might come up on this list and I guarantee that you will find yourself saying to yourself, 'why did I stop doing that?'

Strategic Planning

Clearly, in the Complacency Zone, more drastic and immediate action is required. The world has passed you by and even going back to some of the old ideas that worked might be too late. It's time to consider what's working and what's not and make some strategic decisions of what the future holds. Some things you enjoyed doing may no longer be applicable and fundamental change is required.

The following is a list of some of the areas that you may need to give some new thought to. This may be to either consider and implement new tactics and strategies around them or perhaps redesign or restructure existing plans. It may be as simple as what you could do to even re-invigorate your current activity (or maybe lack of it). This list was compiled with the help of Shirlaws[4] to whom I am grateful.

Re-appraise your Product Offering

This may be the physical product or service you sell, or what it is you do for you occupations. What is it that you are offering that distinguishes you from your competitors?

You must be able to answer the question of what makes you different or even unique.

Re-appraise your Distribution Channel

How do you get your product, service or expertise to the market? It's time for a complete re-evaluation of your sources of distribution and whether they are working effectively and efficiently for you. Maybe you need to explore new avenues, either different ways of distribution and / or who you are selling to; remember, even if you are employed, you are still selling your expertise and value to your employer. Is it the right employer that values your offering?

Re-appraise your Team

Are the right internal and external people and systems deployed to ensure the right person, is

---

[4] Shirlaws is an international business coaching company. I often refer them to our clients to help them get their business on the right track.

doing the right job, at the right time? Is it time to move people around or to recruit new members of your team?

Allied to this is an honest review of what you are doing personally. Are you doing things you should not be doing, both in and outside of your profession?

Are you the right person to be doing some of the activities that would be better delegated to someone else who could do it better or more efficiently than you?

Draw up a list of the things you do in a typical week and then consider who could do those jobs more effectively.

Re-appraise your Management Systems

Ensure that you have systems in place to track and check capability and key performance indicators so that your strategy is a constant evolution rather than a haphazard and intermittent process.

This should be done regularly rather than waiting for a knee jerk reaction to a shock event. Indeed, had you been doing so, then you would not be in the Complacency Zone anyway!

Re-appraise how you can Leverage your Existing Resources

Consider what drivers impact the equity value of the business or your position. That is, rather than just sales now (or being paid for doing a job), what can be done to create brand value or future passive income by taking advantage of your current assets, skills, knowledge and expertise.

By combining these re-appraisals, you will create a personalised strategy for getting yourself out of the Complacency Zone and, hopefully, a re-invigorated new Confidence Zone.

6/ Problems with Goal Achievement

> *"Happiness is not a goal...it's a by-product of a life well lived."*
>
> Eleanor Roosevelt

The reality is that, however much we plan our future strategy, enabled by our pure clarity of vision, there are some of our goals that we will simply not achieve. This 'failure' may occur on a daily basis or over something that may be considered long term. Of course, this should not be thought of as failure, it is just a fact of life that some things may be beyond our actual abilities and some unanticipated changes may occur which ruin our good plans.

We can have all of the best plans and execute them perfectly, yet what we thought was straight-forward often fails to be that. The reality is that human beings do not always act in a rational manner and will make decisions that make no sense to us. There may be factors that we failed to consider or are even beyond our control.

Many people become easily disheartened by this and even suffer deep and long feelings of rejection. These reactions and feelings are classic examples of Glass Ceilings that we impose in our own mind, allied to a Fear of Failure that we may end up repeating this failure. We, naturally, don't want to re-inforce those feelings, so we try to rationalise the failure or lack of achievement. It's human nature to do this whether it's us as individuals or groups, such as the unemployed, who talk about being disenfranchised. And for some, this feeling of oppression from their Glass Ceiling causes them to react and perhaps riot and protest.

I'd like you to imagine the following: wherever you are sitting right now, look out of the window and into the distance. Ignoring any obstructions that might be in the way, what do you see in the far distance? It's the horizon.

Now, I'd like you to imagine getting up out of your seat and setting off on a journey to the horizon; it is an impossible and disillusioning activity. Every time you take a step towards it, the horizon retreats a step back. You can try as hard as you like, and put all the best plans in place for it, but you cannot seem to get there.

Perhaps, we can consider the horizon an analogy for some of our goals, our dreams and aspirations, in particular those that we fail to achieve.

Maybe it is a deal you tried your best to pull off but, for whatever reason, you did your best, but still didn't secure the business. Many people enter a slump at this kind of event, and can stay there for a very long time.

My long-time business coach, Dan Sullivan of The Strategic Coach programme, describes this as **'The Gap'**, the void between our dreams and desires we strive towards and the reality we actually achieve. And The Gap is where many people live their lives, dwelling on their failures and inability to reach their goals. Sometimes, The Gap can appear on an almost daily basis and can be debilitating. However, there is a simply strategy which we can employ to transform this negative energy into a positive experience.

That is, rather than concentrating on what we have failed to achieve, and allowing that sense of failure to dictate our life, we should consider, enjoy and savour where we have come from. We should appreciate the journey from where we started towards our goal, objective or vision and realise that, in the very process of setting those goals and creating that vision and making the changes, we have developed our skill set and grown as individuals. Gratitude and recognition for what we have accomplished are very powerful tools for engendering a sense of positivity. And, in being conscious of our growth, we can create the environment for further growth and development.

Here's an exercise which you could use to habitually and methodically create a sense of positive direction and purpose.

At regular intervals, which could be weekly, monthly or (at the most) quarterly, sit down in a quiet place and review the period since the last time you did this exercise; when doing it for the first time, you may wish to review the previous 12 months as a starting point. During this time of reflection, think about the positive things that have happened to you over that period. These must be things that made you feel good or happy, perhaps events or activities you participated in, skills and knowledge you've learned, qualifications you gained, people you've met that excited you, motivated you or inspired you, perhaps it was securing a new client or professional contact, maybe a promotion or achieving a professional qualification or sales target, possibly a conference you attended, a speech you heard or a book you read that helped you Smash a Glass Ceiling for you.

And they should not just be professional or career related activities, but also things you achieved in your personal life for which you have immense appreciation or gratitude.

Maybe it was a special celebration you had with your family or friends, perhaps a memorable holiday, trip or even family day out, maybe a sporting or other activity, something where you enjoyed feelings of achievement and satisfaction.

Ideally list at least five of each of your career and personal achievements. The point of the exercise is that, in attempting to reach our goals and objectives and failing to do so, we often forget where we started from and what we achieved along the way. By carrying out this 'looking back' exercise and reflecting on the positive results we have achieved, we obtain a rush of positive energy by reliving those experiences.

Before you read on, do the above exercise right now; you could use the tool at the end of this chapter as a guide.

Just by doing this first step, you will feel good and maybe you'll even smile a little when you recall your achievements.

We can use this positive glow as the foundation of some further energising activity (Dan Sullivan calls this exercise 'The Positive Focus') to create some new strategies for the short to medium term, building upon the things we have already enjoyed.

After creating your list, beside each one, write down and acknowledge why it was important to you. Having recognised and appreciated its importance, next write down what is the further development required to move that event to an even higher level or even to simply repeat the activity again; for example, you went to the theatre to see a play, really enjoyed it and would like to see another.

Convert this desire into action by writing down the very first step required to enable the strategy. Quite often, if we take the first step, the rest will happen but failing to start, means the project just lingers regretfully.

The final two things to write down are 'who is involved' and 'by when'. Everything does not have to be done by ourselves but could be delegated to others such as our staff, our team or members of our family. Giving the first step a deadline gives it momentum, energy and a genuine sense of urgency.

The Positive Focus is a very powerful tool for dealing with The Gap, re-energising ourselves for the continued long haul by appreciating and recognising the valuable events that uplift us. The Gap seems irrelevant afterwards and I urge you to try is as a written down exercise.

You could use the tool on the next page; email me and I'll send it to you, to print out and regularly update.

FOCUSING ON SUCCESS - A QUARTERLY REVIEW

Step 1: What great events have happened in the past 3 months that were important, memorable or exciting? What motivated you and energised you and why?

Step 2: What do you need to do to build upon that?

Step 3: Who do you need to help you?

Step 4: What's the first step and by when?

Event	Why is it Important?	Further Progress	Who's Involved?	First Step	By When?

7/ The Transition from "Can't" to "Let me Show you How?"

> *"The only person who can pull me down is myself, and I'm not going to let myself pull me down anymore."*
>
> C. TovBell, C.

Having set up some themes about what is involved in recognising our Glass Ceilings, knowing that they are largely dictated by our attitudes towards them and issues that arise such as the Three Cs and The Gap in addressing our Glass Ceilings, I'd now like to share some anecdotes with you about Glass Ceilings that I have faced and how I have dealt with them.

I previously stated that I am no-one special and have no distinct skills or expertise greater than you, dear reader, and I stand by that. And I do hope that, through sharing these stories and my attitude towards Glass Ceilings, you may identify with some of the barriers you too may be facing and may find encouragement, perhaps even inspiration, from my experiences.

I have been very fortunate to have experienced some pretty amazing things in my life. I have always thought they just happened through circumstance, co-incidence or, indeed, just plain good luck.

As I have reflected deeply upon some of those moments and learned more about definitions of success, and considered the opinion and comments of others about me, I have come to realise that many of those events were as a result of my attitude. An attitude that challenges the norm and established conventions and does not accept the first answer that is given, but tries to explore new alternative solutions. This attitude has now become a habit.

All of us, of course, learn through life's experiences, through both successes and, more importantly, through the mistakes we invariably make. But, how many of us stop to actively digest those experiences to consider the impact they make?

One of the things that I have now, upon reflection, realised about myself is that when someone or circumstances say that I can't do something, I simply don't hear those words or their negative connotation. My brain doesn't digest the word 'can't' and instead interprets it as a challenge, reframing the words as 'so when are you going to try?' Alternatively, my reaction is 'Ok, that's what you think. Let me show you how!'

That doesn't mean that I go out to deliberately

break rules or be obstructive, but it does mean that, if I don't believe something to be correct, then I will challenge that situation to the best of my ability. I am not argumentative for the sake of it (although I often enjoy playing devil's advocate [5]), but I am certainly demanding. My clients have told me that that is a quality they like in me, to stand up for their position when necessary and to ask the sometimes awkward and difficult questions that I would ask if I were them.

My team know that if they research an answer (perhaps from an insurance company or other product provider) to a query from me, they had better think carefully about the response they are given and pre-empt what the next question will be if it is not the answer I want, as I will only send them back to carry our further due diligence.

It is a characteristic that has stood me well and kept us at the forefront of product innovation. Providers that we work with are constantly saying that 'no-one has asked that question before' when, for me, it is usually an obvious question that needed to be asked and I am surprised that no-one has previously raised the same query.. I used to

---

[5] Devil's Advocate: A person who expresses a contentious opinion in order to provoke debate or test the strength of the opposing arguments.

take this for granted, thinking that everyone must be thinking this way, but it happens so frequently that I have to declare that I am a complete maverick[6] (which is fine by me) or maybe just a trouble-maker! I can honestly say that it is the mark of a successful individual to never accept things the way that they are, and to challenge conventions; as an example, I will talk later about how people are instigators of change or the recipients of change and that how that is a pro-active choice to be made. Indeed, I have already hopefully got you thinking about this in the previous chapter about the 'Three Cs'.

In the meantime, a test for you would be to start questioning customs and conventions more often. If you don't like the answer you get, think about what can be done to get the solution you desire. Make it a habit.

If someone says something can't be done (unless you accept it is impossible) spend more time than you normally would, considering what needs to happen for the ideal solution to occur.

Whenever you hear someone saying that 'it can't be done', take it as a personal challenge for you to prove it can. You won't always win your point, but

---

[6] Maverick: an independent thinker who refuses to conform to the accepted views on a subject

you will be surprised at what change you can cause and influence along the way. In doing so, not only do you liberate yourself and raise your confidence, you also do this for the people around you who are also intellectually stimulated by this behaviour.

Someone saying 'can't' to you is an example of the imposition of a Glass Ceiling. It is your *own* attitude and reaction to it that will determine the outcome, not that other person's opinion.

Indeed, with the benefit of personal hindsight and deep contemplation, I can now take a considered look at some of my past experiences in order to make judgements about occasions where I have faced Glass Ceilings imposed by others, and I have chosen to Smash those obstructions. At such times, it was not necessarily a conscious decision on my behalf, but it was an attitude and behaviour that made the word (or concept) of 'can't do something' seem like a Glass Ceiling that was not going to last for long. Each of these Glass Ceilings was a challenge that I relished, although at the time, it didn't always feel like it!

I want to share with you what incredible things can happen when you have the courage to break through the Glass Ceiling. I'd like you to accompany me on my personal journey, to learn the importance of clear vision and breaking barriers. In sharing these experiences, I hope that you may take some of the ideas and techniques and apply them to your life.

In relating some of these forthcoming anecdotes, I recognise that it may appear to some that I am boasting of some relatively small personal achievements. That is certainly not the case. I am merely using some real life experiences to explain what can happen when we have a clear vision and sense of pride of who we are and what we stand for. Not everything I do is perfect and if I started listing all of my imperfections, they would certainly exceed my achievements but they would also not serve to motivate or inspire you, which is my prime purpose.

I do not claim to have achieved any major sporting record or been an extreme explorer or overcome any disability; others may use these to share their experience as a form of motivation or inspiration for others.

The achievements that I am about to share are much, much smaller by comparison, but they were significant for me.

The real message behind what I am going to relate is how Glass Ceilings need to be recognised and then how they can be Smashed and, importantly, that you could do the very same.

I am most definitely no-one special, and rest assured that I have the same size brain as you with the very same abilities. I just have a willingness to share some ideas and concepts that have worked for me that will also work for you if you are prepared to put the effort in to make the required changes.

Of course, you can choose not to put in the effort, that being your prerogative. All I can say is that, through speeches to many thousands of delegates all around the globe, the feedback I get that my stories have helped to change other peoples' lives for the better motivates me to do more.

Remember, the theme of many of these anecdotes is a prevailing attitude of substituting the word 'can't' for 'when will you try' or 'let me show you how'.

8 / My Entry to the World of Finance

> *"Why are you trying so hard to fit in, when you're born to stand out."*
>
> *Oliver James*

I opened this book by declaring that I have always wanted to be a financial advisor. This choice of career arose due to one man that inspired me to believe that this is one of the most honourable of all professions.

Brian Morley was a life insurance agent for Sun Life of Canada throughout the 1970s and has since, unsurprisingly, progressed to senior management positions within that esteemed company.

He was also my father's insurance agent and was a role model for me. I remember him as a child, visiting my home and talking to my father about his future. He was smart and articulate and my father had complete confidence in him. He bought life insurance and investments from him and when he was ready to set up his own business, it was Brian who helped my father raise a loan and establish his first retail venture.

I didn't realise it at the time (and I don't think he did either!), but Brian made an impact upon me; he instilled a belief in me that being an insurance agent is one of the most noble of professions that commands the utmost respect. Of course I believed that (and still do), as it was Brian's guiding hand that carefully steered my father to ever greater success. Brian would be invited to family gatherings and my father would always proudly introduce him to all his friends. Although I admired Brian immensely, I really didn't realise the subconscious impact it was having upon me at the time.

In fact, insurance wasn't my anticipated career choice as I believed that I had an aptitude for the practical and studied Mechanical Engineering at Oxford Polytechnic (now Oxford Brookes University). I disliked my course, and wasn't a great academic, but loved my time as a student life.

I was very active and involved in many aspects of student life, including chairing various societies, being a DJ and working behind the bar (little did I realise this would come in useful in a future job interview as I will explain in a later chapter!). It was clear to me that my true aptitude was actually people-oriented, which engineers generally are not. I preferred to organise events and activities rather than be immersed in the finer details of fluid thermodynamics.

I recall that one of the lecturers was a world authority on glue (I guess someone has to be!). He would get excited about the interaction of polymers, atoms and molecules in adhesive technology, but, frankly, I didn't want to stick with it (pun intended!)

As I take you through a short history of my career, you may start to notice a trend of non-conformity, a way of thinking which doesn't always mean that you are right, it's just that you have a stance, an opinion on things and are prepared to think in an alternative way. Always, pushing for change and never accepting the first option that is provided. Even so, there are ethics and morals of 'doing the right thing' and standing up for principles.

Is this attitude something you can learn or is it natural? I believe you can learn it and adopt it and make it your own. Indeed, as a child I was shy and relatively introvert, but gradually realised that that is not how I wished to remain.

For example, after my final year as a student, I took a year out in a sabbatical post as Treasurer of the Oxford Brookes Students' Union. My parents did not want me to do this and considered it as a waste of time, but I perceived it as an opportunity to grow my talents and to distance myself from engineering, a career I was definitely not going to follow. It turned out to be one of the best and character forming years of my life.

I worked with a great committee and it was my first

opportunity to use my inherent entrepreneurial skills. With a turnover of £1 million, there was huge responsibility in running this as a serious business. Sadly, the year before had been negligent in this process and we sat on a large deficit. It was going to be a tough year!

As with any business, I took stock of where we were and prepared a cash-flow projection for the year; cuts were going to have to be made across the board and we would also have to think up new ways of creating new revenue, perhaps through better management of existing resources. These early experiences helped and shaped my future business acumen. Upon reflection, as a Union we were in a Complacency Zone and dramatic change was required.

Having been proactive in student activities, I had developed a reputation as someone who could hold an audience with a captivating speech. There was plenty of opportunity to practice these skills (which, at the time, I took for granted, not realising what great benefit it was creating for my future) and I was often asked to chair important meetings and conferences and to participate in them. One of my biggest speeches was at the National Union of Students Annual Conference in Blackpool in front of several thousand delegates. Strangely, I enjoyed it despite the terror of the experience!

However successful we were in our revenue generating endeavours, we were still short of funds. Seeing that we were heading for trouble, I was tasked by the executive committee to approach the Governors of the University for further funding. This may sound like a simple formality, but this was the mid-1980s and there was a desperate shortage of money in higher education. The university was struggling to work within its own budget and the local authority was virtually bankrupt. I was given an impossible task. Looking back on it now, it was a form of Glass Ceiling. I could have declined to tackle the problem, seeing what we wanted and needed but giving in to the reality of the situation that I was going to have to do something impossible. I am no magician, but I reluctantly took on the challenge.

Preparation was crucial and this has been a lesson that has been key throughout my life and career. I do as much preparation as possible for a presentation, and the way to do it effectively is to do something that I find very few people doing; put yourself in the shoes of the person or audience that you are talking to.

Who are they and what is their background and experience? What will they want to know from me and what are the questions, objections and challenges they are likely to bring up? Run through the meeting in your mind and visualise what is going to happen. The more detailed you can be in this analysis, the better will be the actual outcome.

Again, this is not rocket science, it is a simple strategy that is so easy to do but most people don't. Next time you are going to give any kind of presentation, large or small, verbal or written, ask yourself the following question: 'Based upon who I am and what I know, if I was in the audience listening to me, what would I want to know that would help me move forward and make a plan or a decision?'

I prepared for that meeting by researching who each of the members of the Board of Governors were, what their backgrounds were and what they might know about the Students' Union. The Board was made up, not just of academics and University staff, but by local politicians, local authority heads, various business people and other dignitaries and VIPs.

They didn't necessarily all know what we did and the value we provided for the students and the importance of the role we played in their lives. I'm sure that many of them thought that we were either just hardened, radical political activists organising marches and sit-ins or organising social events for students to get drunk as cheaply as possible, there being an element of truth in those assumptions!

A Side-note on the Preparation

I will bring this up again later, but one of the easiest steps in Preparation is to put yourself in the shoes of your audience.

As a member of the audience, what is it that you already know and what is it that you need or want to know from the presentation in order to make an informed decision?

Too many times, I see presenters making assumptions about their audience (even in a one-to-one meeting) that they have a certain level of knowledge or expertise in the subject, which is not necessarily the case; that it why you are there.

For example, walk through your office as if you were visiting it for the first time and think about the first impressions that are being made. Analyse your presentation materials. They may look good to you, but that's because you understand them. How could you simplify things?

I prepared a full analysis of what we did and made it easy to understand, and explained in full what we needed the money for and the severe impact of not getting it. It was, in theory, a perfect sales pitch!

I took two other members of the executive with me for moral support, to face what was a daunting and monumental task. As I walked along the imposing corridor of power and entered the silent boardroom, with grim faces staring at me as if I was coming to steal their precious treasure, I felt like I was a character in 'The Lord of the Rings'. They had the Ring of cash and, like Gollum, I wanted my hand on it. This was going to be terrifying and as our item on the agenda drew ever closer, my palms became sweaty and my mouth dry as the moment of truth arrived.

I passed out some handouts and then took the Board through a synopsis of what we did, laying on thickly the impact of the lack of funding. I ensured that I made eye contact with every person in this room of intense silence and contemplation and got them nodding their heads in understanding. Incredibly, there was only one question, which I batted back with confidence. The dearth of questions made me feel that the Board had already decided against us and was just going through there motions

As I sat down, I looked at my colleagues who gave me a wry smile as if they knew something I didn't. They had clearly been reading the faces of the Governors better than I had. We waited patiently for the Chair take a vote and, as we held our breath, dreading the outcome, there was, unbelievably, unanimous approval for our request.

The bottom line is that there were only nominal objections and, even though they did not have the money, we moved the problem of what impact it would have on to the Board and they gave us the funding. My team later told me that they thought it was the speech of a lifetime. Perhaps this was a subliminal endorsement that has sat as a guide and reinforcement in my subconscious ever since.

I was fêted as a hero, but there was a big lesson about the power of good preparation here which has stood me in good stead ever since. It also showed that there is no Glass Ceiling that cannot be Smashed, whatever the odds against it happening.

Perhaps it is just fantastic preparation and clear visualisation of the outcome that is needed for you to face your Glass Ceilings and move towards Smashing them. There will be more tools to follow, but that is a good starting point.

After leaving University, I recalled my feelings about my father's insurance agent, Brian Morley. I felt that this was a respected career path to follow and started to explore it further. The sabbatical year had suitably distanced me from engineering.

In particular, I secured an interview to become an insurance agent for Liberty Life in their Regent Street, London office. As I waited patiently in the room where several candidates were gathered, the sales manager talked about some of the successful individuals in the office and, in particular, mentioned an unusual name who I knew as a fellow student at Oxford Brookes. I was surprised to hear of his success as, at the university, he was considered by many to be weird and a loner. He did not have many friends and led a strange lifestyle. But here he was, as a top agent, making a fortune. Great, I thought, if he can do it, surely so can I.

I proceeded with the interview, which seemed to go very well and then had to sit an aptitude test. You know, the ones where you are asked a series of questions to assess your attitude towards particular issues, in order for a computer to assess your multiple choice answers and come up with a formal description or assessment about you. There can never be a wrong answer and there is no pass or fail, it merely attempts to describe your character.

I failed the test!

The sales manager said that the aptitude test had declared me to be too nice for this job! He said that the insurance industry was not for me and that I would never be successful in this business and that I should look for a career in some other industry. Wow, I thought, I did not know that it was a problem being too nice for a job that needs you to be friendly with people and develop long-term relationships. Maybe that is why my friend from the university was doing so well, as it seemed that he treated it as a ruthless business that had nothing to do with the normal rules of decency. In which case, it was not a company I wished to work for.

Years later, I'd like to meet that manager today! I'm still enjoying success in this great profession (for which I am apparently too nice) and his company no longer has a sales force and developed a reputation of the worst kind of insurance agent. It was a lucky escape and I feel very happy that I failed that aptitude test.

At the time, however, it set my ambitions back a little. I could have accepted his opinion and chosen a different career but, instead, this was just the first of several career Glass Ceilings that I decided needed to be shattered. It would have been very easy to choose an alternative direction, but I had set my heart on this sector and I was not to be deterred so easily.

I still believed that I had an affinity to the financial services profession, maybe I just needed more experience. So, I applied for and gained the position of a trainee manager for the Leeds Permanent Building Society, a form of bank or savings and loans institution.

Here would be an opportunity to use my entrepreneurial skills and initiative to help the

Society grow. This seemed to work and after just three months, they made me an assistant branch manager.

One day, I was asked to go to the head office in Leeds for some training and, when there, I kept getting some strange looks from senior staff. I asked one of the managers what the problem was and he said that there was no problem, it was just that I was the very first person that the Society had taken on that had a beard! It was apparently an unwritten rule that no-one in management was allowed to grow facial hair and that I was the first person to break this rule. Unwittingly, my maverick tendencies were coming to the fore. It was my first experience of what goes on in a large, established, corporation and it would not be my last. But it was the mid-1980s and I was happy to be breaking an institutionalised Glass Ceiling.

My rapid move into management was eye-opening. I quickly realised that, actually, initiative and 'out of the box' thinking was frowned upon within the organisation. This was a 'dead man's shoes' business; we all had to wait for someone at the top to die or retire and then we all moved up one rung on the ladder. That was the way it had always been and a maverick like me was a troublemaker. I was deemed to be overdemanding, but, nevertheless garnered respect as I always had a valid point, it's just that the wheels of progress were too slow in turning. For example, we did not have a photocopier in the branch in which I worked, which meant that we had to take confidential documents to the local copy-shop for copying. This frustrated me no end and I used to complain about this and similar inefficiencies vigorously. Nevertheless, someone higher up saw potential in me and a year later, I was offered the post of a branch manager. This was now time for a strategic review of my career.

Before I go on to that, I should say that one of the attitudes of success that I maintain is to always be the best at what you do. Now, 'best' is an arbitrary value (although there are ways of measuring it through competitions and awards), but there are still some basic standards. In my opinion, one of these is to gain the relevant qualifications in whatever your profession or trade is. Very early on in my career at 'The Leeds', I made a conscious decision that if this was to be my lifetime career, then be the best at it and obtain the most suitable qualifications. So I started studying for the Chartered Building Society Institute examinations. Others frowned upon this as being unnecessary and so why do things you don't have to do. I could have adhered to their mini-Glass Ceilings and gone with the flow, but I had bigger objectives in mind. The theme behind this is that, in any profession, minimum qualification levels only go up, never down. So, why wait for those new minimum standards to be raised, get there first.

A Side-Note on the Concept of 'Best'

In the next few chapters, I want to explore the concept of 'best' a little more.

For now though, allow me to ask you a question which goes to the heart of your mind-set. Make sure you answer the following question with the first thought that comes into your head. If you think about the answer, you will fail to capture the essence and immediacy of the answer.

In your profession, do you believe that there is anyone better than you?

What was your answer? There is no right or wrong, just a reflection of how you see yourself amongst your peer group.

Now, if I was a prospect and you were courting me for your business, how would you answer if I asked you, 'Are you the best that there is or is there anyone better I should be talking to?'

Did your answer change?

I've tested this with numerous people and it is interesting how their answer to the first question was a little vague or unsure. Yet, when it makes a potential difference to their pocket, it seems that their confidence level goes sky high and they are suddenly the very best!

Why should it have to be any different depending upon who you are talking to or what it might be worth to you? If you genuinely have the self-belief, then it is not arrogance, but supreme confidence that allows you to express your conviction.

And if you don't really feel that confident, then answering that question to a prospect (or perhaps an employer) will come across as disingenuous and lacking in assurance.

Think about this point very carefully as the core of demonstrating your confidence.

At that time, The Leeds was an independent financial advisory firm and, as such, we had representatives of various insurance companies who would come to visit us to peddle their wares. These 'broker consultants' would try to encourage us to use their services for when we were selling life insurance, endowment plans or pensions to our mortgage customers. I recall looking at some of these individuals who had a big expense account, a company car, lots of freedom and were earning more than me and yet had very little inter-personal skills or technical competence. Many times, I would deliberately learn new things and then challenge these consultants on their knowledge of their own products and industry trends and they really struggled to engage intellectually. It wasn't long before I resented some of these people and started to feel that I could do their job better than them.

Being offered my own branch to manage was the catalyst for change. I knew that if I stayed at The Leeds, I would be sucked into the corporate machine and stuck on the long-term ladder. It would then need a pay cut to take a different job, which would be harder, so the offer of higher management made me apply for jobs as a Broker Consultant with some leading life offices and, before long I had several offers in my hand from some major insurers.

However, one company that I applied to was challenging me and I made it a mission to take that one, even if it set me back another year. There were some personal principles at stake and, upon reflection, it taught me some very valuable lessons.

I was also about to face an unbelievable Glass Ceiling...

9/ The 'Triumph over Evil'

> *"How people treat you is their karma; how you react is yours."*
>
> Wayne W. Dyer

Having secured job offers from three other companies, my preferred company, Scottish Equitable (now known as Aegon), was taking a long time in making progress. They were dragging the process out for no discernible reason...although I was to shortly find out why.

Eventually, after two interviews that seemed to go very well, for a job as a broker consultant working out of the Harrow office in North West London, I was asked to see the London area staff manager, an elderly chap by the name of John Wilkinson. In those days (the late 1980s), it was very rare for a traditional British life office to sack anyone. Instead, if someone was not quite up to the standard any longer, they would be given a quiet, unexceptional, role of little influence until they reached retirement age. John Wilkinson was one of those. He was very much of the old-school type and it was clear that his job did not exist before him and, tellingly, he was not replaced when he finally retired. No-one really knew what he did, but he wanted to meet me for a third interview.

No problem, I thought. Even though it was strange to need a third interview, I was summoned to see John, who had never needed to interview broker consultants in his role before. Before going, I was warned by the Harrow branch manager, Chris Anderton, that this would be no ordinary interview. He told me that it was unfortunate that, in its 160 year history, Scottish Equitable had very rarely, if ever, employed someone from an ethnic minority, especially in a sales role and that I was the first that he knew of. As such, John Wilkinson had got to hear of it and started to create a fuss as if this would be the downfall of the insurance company, being dragged kicking and screaming into the 20th Century cosmopolitan world.

I could not believe that such bigoted views still existed and it sounded like he seemed like a relic of the apartheid system in South Africa which I had so actively campaigned against as a student. I could have walked away from this issue, but I decided that I was not going to feel threatened and that John Wilkinson was about to meet his match!

I honestly thought that these types of Glass Ceilings had been destroyed decades before, but when I met this man for the interview, he tried to intimidate me with his racist ignorance. I could tell from his eyes that he had already made up his mind about me and decided that his role was now to somehow prevent me from being offered this job, by tripping me up with some pretty naïve views and irrelevant questions. Indeed, his questions said more about his character and his attitude than drawing out any real insights from me.

But pride of who we are and what we stand for creates strength of character and I totally refused to be bullied. In fact, I treated this as an opportunity to expose John's outrageous bigotry and narrow mindedness.

I walked into the interview room with my chest high but still some nervous trepidation as to what to expect. There was no pleasant smile on his part as I sat down and just the most formal of welcomes. He had my file on his desk as I took my seat across his great wooden desk and started to flick through the papers in an effort to distract me with his silence. I looked around the room and waited patiently for him to start the game. In fact, instead of the silence being threatening, I used it as time for me relax and force a smile on my face. This seemed to disarm John as I think he thought I should be sweating nervously.

We started the interview with some normal chitchat about past experience, hobbies, experience for the role and other small talk, none of which he really showed any enthusiasm or interest in.

Having run out of the usual thing to say, he

suddenly came out with, 'So, you're a Sikh.'

Here we go, I thought. 'Very observant of you', I replied, just a little sarcastically.

He coughed a little nervously and then continued, 'Being a Sikh, how will you get on with people of other religions you will meet when doing your job? Won't that be a barrier?' he questioned.

I nearly fell off my chair! I was so taken aback and disgusted that he was even suggesting such a thing. I responded resolutely, 'John, let me inform you that I have absolutely no issues with anyone of any other race, colour, creed, sexuality or religion. I celebrate the diversity of people and always look for the good in people'.

I looked him straight in the eye and firmly continued, 'You should not presume that all other people necessarily carry such prejudice and discrimination with them and, actually, if you personally have any problems with this, perhaps you would like to talk about it. I'm a good listener'. I decided that this conversation was going to be fun! I had nothing to lose, and my character, confidence and self-belief were now becoming powerful tools.

He flustered on. 'So, you're a Sikh' he started.

'Yes, we've already established that', I interrupted indignantly.

'So, as a Sikh, you don't drink alcohol and this job requires you to do a lot of socialising, so how will you be able to cope with that?' This was an interesting line of questioning and most unusual.

'Well', I replied, the disdain in my tone becoming more noticeable. 'Since when does being sociable necessitate drinking alcohol?' I was now in full flow!

'Believe it or not, John, I am perfectly capable of holding a conversation and having a lot of fun without the need to be inebriated; it's a useful skill, perhaps you should try it sometime', I suggested to him sarcastically. He seemed visibly shocked that I was not being intimidated by him, so I continued to turn the knife. 'However, as you bring up the subject, I used to work behind the bar as a student and learned lots of drinking games through my friends in the rugby club, and I would be happy to teach you some if you want!'

This guy clearly had some bizarre views and opinions, treating anyone not like him as if they were an alien. The interview carried on in the same vein for some time, as if it was a swordfight, with each of John's attacks being parried with a sharp poke back. I refused to give any ground, playing from a position of strength, knowing that other offers were already in my hands.

By the end of it, John seemed more exhausted than

I did and I left with a smile on my face and a deep frown of indignation on his. As we parted, he threw in one more sly comment, 'May I compliment you on your English, you speak it very well'.

Wow, I thought, what an idiot. He knew that I had lived in Britain since I was ten months old, so what did he expect? I had to get the last word in, so I replied, 'Thank you...and so do you, John'. He was not happy!

I subsequently even saw a letter he hand wrote to the National Sales Manager, John Elliott, (who was just as bad as him) in which he stated that, "This man is a Sikh and wears a turban, but speaks perfect English". (And since when was that a crime?). "He is not teetotal, and claims to get on with all nationalities and races. In fact, I could not find any fault with him and therefore we have no choice but to reluctantly accept him".

Incredibly, I later found out that my simple job application had reached the agenda of the Board of directors of Scottish Equitable. To their credit and, as a result of lobbying from Chris Anderton and the company's Human Resources manager, it was quite rightly thrown off the agenda. I have always admired Chris for his faith in me and not just taking the easy line. It was clear to me that this was not a corporate line or institutionalised racism, just the ignorance of one or two people in senior positions.

Eventually, Scottish Equitable issued me an offer of employment to go alongside the others I also had from other more enlightened companies. With a toughened Glass Ceiling above me, I could have chosen the easy life and accepted one of the other offers in my hand. Or, I could take the difficult route and challenge this racism and prejudice head on.

My family and friends were urging to me accept one of the other job offers that I held in my grasp, but something inside me was enraged by the situation. I could not stand by and simply let such crass and offensive behaviour win. This had become a clear matter of principle for me.

The philosopher, Edmund Burke, once said that "all that is necessary for evil to triumph is that good men do nothing". Perhaps as a result of my faith, my upbringing or my education (and possibly all of these), I believe that it is important to stand up proudly for one's own morals and principles. Out of all the offers I held, this was the one I wanted, I had something to prove and I wanted to break the stereotypical images that these people held. I did not consider John Wilkinson to be evil, but I did consider his views to be vile.

Despite pleas from family and friends not to, I joined Scottish Equitable as a broker consultant and began servicing a neglected panel of Independent Financial Advisors in North / North-West London.

10/ The Downfall from Top Ten...and Back Up Again

> *"Our greatest glory is not in never falling, but in rising every time we fall."*
>
> Confucius

The broker consultant job involved me visiting a diverse range of financial advisors to promote Scottish Equitable's products and to encourage them to use our products when advising their clients. I was given a target and, as well as a basic salary, car and benefits, I was rewarded with bonuses based upon my production. This was a good opportunity to exploit my entrepreneurial flair, as I was responsible for managing my own time and deciding who I wanted to see and helping them to write more business.

It also gave me a great and meaningful insight into the different types of firms operating in this sector; I didn't realise it at the time, but this was going to prove invaluable in my later career. What became very clear was that some of these firms were one-man band operations, perhaps working out of a spare room in their own home, and others were large businesses with many advisors working as a sales-force, with a wide variation in between. They had different levels of experience and a variety of support needs. Some were very pro-active and hungry for business and others did not really know where their next slice of income was coming from. Some specialised in market sectors and some specialised in product areas.

It was also very interesting bumping into my competitor broker consultants representing other companies. Some of them found the job easy and enjoyable, whilst others struggled to create strong relationships with their panel, and there was always a friendly rivalry between those of us who were doing well.

This experience of dealing with different people, their attitudes (to success and failure), their professionalism (or lack of, in some cases) and their willingness and desire to work with broker consultants who carried a sense of self-confidence, was a great foundation for a future career as a financial advisor. When we deal with clients (whether as a financial advisor or in any other career sector), we deal with people of differing attitudes, various levels of professionalism but they all have a desire to work with advisors who in turn carry a sense of self-confidence and belief.

My experience and confidence in arranging mortgages and raising finance had been obtained through my training at the Leeds Building Society.

Through those contacts and experience, I was able to offer my panel of advisors an unrivalled level of service. In some cases, I was able to produce a mortgage offer in a day! I could pick up an application with all the required supporting documentation from the broker in the morning, instruct the surveyor (to carry out a property valuation) immediately, and by the time I got to the branch office of the building society in the afternoon, the valuation would have been faxed over and I could get an offer printed that day. The spin off was that my firm picked up the associated insurance policy where I earned my credit. Another great lesson about how people value extraordinary service was being learned.

Within the first year of the job, I was in the top ten of Scottish Equitable's broker consultants and number one in my grade. I was loving my job and, above all, I had Smashed the Glass Ceiling! In fact, when John Wilkinson visited our branch for a routine (and totally irrelevant) staff meeting, I took the opportunity to confront him directly and asked him if my manager's faith in me had been vindicated. John spluttered a garbled response that it was never in doubt but, from that day on, he knew that I knew what had happened and he finally began to give me the respect I felt I deserved.

Similarly, on a visit to head office in Edinburgh, I met John Elliot, the National Sales Manager and I took great pleasure in staring at him as he attempted to glare at me furiously in a feeble form of contempt. I wasn't gloating about my position but was more interested in showing these people that their feeble attempt to intimidate me with their Glass Ceiling had failed dismally.

Things were going very well, but in my third year in the job, my world started to crumble. I had become entrenched in my speciality of mortgages and had failed to see what was going on around me. Scottish Equitable had progressively and successfully re-positioned itself as a major pensions provider while the housing market boom had turned into a vicious housing bust. Values were falling, no-one was interested in buying property, the mortgage market died and I had simply not seen it coming. And my lack of pensions knowledge was now beginning to show, as I had little else to talk about.

I now know in hindsight that I had entered a new Confidence Zone a couple of years earlier, success had manoeuvred me into a Comfort Zone and, through lack of awareness, I had gradually slid into a Complacency Zone. And, as I stated in an earlier chapter, this is a very dangerous place to be, as I was about to find out.

From being a top ten broker consultant, my production took a massive dive and I steadily worked my way down the rankings. Eventually, my manager, Chris, had no choice but to issue me with a written warning, to get my figures up...or to get out!

It was at this very point that I realised that it's only 18 inches between a slap on the back or kick up the backside! A written warning certainly tends to concentrate the mind. I had to re-evaluate what I was doing and to make a strategic decision. It was no good blaming the world for having changed, I had to take responsibility for not changing with it.

Consider this for a moment. Who do you blame when things don't go to plan? Sure, sometimes there is something or someone to blame, but often it is because we allowed it to happen. Change will happen, it cannot be resisted, but to be ignorant of change is no-one else's fault but our own. And, as I stated earlier, success lies in being the instigator of change not the recipient or victim of change.

My re-evaluation of what was going on started with a position of denial of responsibility, as if it was the world conspiring against me; it was not my fault.

As I was going through this process of self-mourning, I happened to be watching a golf match on TV.

As I studied these players attempting to outplay each other, a moment of self-realisation struck me. These were all world class players, they were all individually great at what they do yet, at any moment, for no apparent reason, they could play a

110

bad shot. From a field-leading position, they could quickly drop down the ranks. It was as if all the various hazards on the course were conspiring to defeat them; the long grass, the trees, the lakes and the bunker were all traps for those who failed to avoid them.

But, did this mean the game was lost? No! It just meant that the next few shots had to be even better, even more focussed and carefully selected to get back in the game.

In fact, as I contemplated it further, the game would be pretty boring without the hazards to negotiate. Indeed, this was a good analogy for life itself. The hazards of life are not obstacles but they are challenges that have to be tackled. I realised that I was stuck in a very deep bunker and that the next shot I played had to be perfect. Time was running out fast and I was given just three months to turn my production figures around. As with the golfer, I had to take account of my situation and come out fighting with a strategy for success.

I asked myself, what were my strengths and what were my weaknesses? After careful reflection, I identified that my strengths were the relationships I had developed with my panel of advisors who liked me and trusted me. They were also suffering from the extreme change in the market and were looking for support. I enjoyed my job and I had proven to be good at it, but my weakness was my knowledge, particularly in the area of pensions. I had neglected this subject as something I should have developed whilst in my Comfort Zone, but now being in the Complacency Zone required a crash course for results. I realised that I could leverage the relationship that I still had by sharing the knowledge as I acquired it, and I could also add my personal twist to it by showing advisors how to sell more pensions.

I created a game plan for instant results. I signed up for every available pensions course and read every related article on the subject. Phrases that, before, were complete jargon to me, began to make sense and, fairly rapidly, I began to apply these new found skills. My production turned around and was back on the rise and, shortly thereafter, the warning notice was lifted, the Glass Ceiling it had created was Smashed! In fact, I steadily climbed up the rankings again and soon afterwards, I was one of the top three broker consultants at the company.

There were many lessons learned during this process, many of which have proved useful in my later career.

Firstly, always be aware of the change that is happening around you. To neglect change is like a golfer who constantly hits the ball into the trees on purpose. It would be a ridiculous thing to do.

More so, rather than just observing change, be part of the change. What I mean by that is to anticipate the changes that are likely to happen and create a strategy that is ahead of the change. In this way, rather than being the recipients of change, we can become the instigators or influencers and victims of change.

Let's take an example of an Olympic high jump competition. In any of these competitions, the bar is set at a particular height and raised 1cm at a time and all the competitors are eliminated as and when they fail to pass the new height. But, there is always one of the jumpers who observes the others and, at an opportune moment, raises the bar more than 1cm. As he does so, he has 'raised the bar' through his own self-belief and confidence that he can reach that height.

Think about your role in your career. Are you one of those who watches others raising the bar and wonder why you didn't see it coming? Or, do you have examples of where you did something so radically different, unusual or unexpected that it left others so bemused and confused they did not know how to compete. It could be, for example, gaining new qualifications, sourcing a new stream of business, an innovative use of technology or a creative marketing strategy; the list is endless, but true and lasting success belongs to those who constantly raise the bar.

Another lesson learned was that instead of always looking for the easy way out, it's vital to challenge ourselves, in order to reach incredible new heights.

In taking on the job at Scottish Equitable, I had challenged myself and taken a gamble. The world may have been conspiring against me, but my attitude towards it was that we can all change the world, bit by bit, but only if we have the courage to try. What is *your* attitude towards the obstacles and hazards that will come your way? Do you run scared of them, to take the easy route out, do you ignore them and hope that it has no effect on you or do you challenge them straight on? Remember, it is our attitude to these Glass Ceilings that determines how effectively we are able to deal with them.

Another valuable lesson learned was that when we face Glass Ceilings imposed upon us by others, we complain, yet when those Glass Ceilings are self-imposed through our limiting beliefs...we still blame others. It's a common excuse to say 'it's not my fault', 'the world is not fair'. But, the real question is, what are we going to do about it? I had painfully learned that, sometimes, business is easy, but it's not *always* easy.

Equally, sometimes business is difficult, but it's not *always* difficult. The difference is in our attitude of what changes we are prepared to make when the difficulties do arise.

I realised that strong and valued relationships were a key to sustained success. I had stood by my panel of advisors as they underwent change (and some did not survive this change) and, in turn, they stood by me. They were having to go through similar changes and were happy that I was there alongside them. It taught me a crucial lesson that people don't buy products, people buy people.

I realised that it did not matter whether Scottish Equitable had the best products or not, my panel would always factor into the advice to their clients the quality of the service they obtained from a product provider as a key feature of their product selection. I respected my panel of advisors as being business people and was constantly aware that, if I was going to see them, I would have to add value to what they were doing. I never saw these advisors to talk about my products. I wanted to know about them, their current business strategy and their future plans. I wanted to know about their clients, what they did for them and what they would like to do with them further. This focus on *them* rather than my products was going to be powerful learning experience for later in my career, when I would be seeing my own clients and is something I always talk about in my presentations.

These advisors knew that a meeting with me would result in them making more money. I used to say that I would help them manage their sales process by only meeting with them if they pulled out at least five client files each time for us to profile and explore new planning opportunities. I soon reached a position where my panel of advisors, which started at over 150, had been reduced down to around just five key players and about ten other supporters. Between them, it meant that instead of being on a warning, I was steadily sustaining 160% of my business target. To put that in perspective, the company at that time was only achieving 75% of its corporate target.

Another lesson for the future was my experience of the Pareto principle – 80% of the reward comes from just 20% of the people and in my case it was more like a 90/10 ratio. I did not need to chase all 150 advisors on my panel, I only needed to have great relationships with a few who were writing lots of business. These people got more of my time and attention and deservedly so. The balance knew who I was and what I was offering, but I took the view that not dealing with me was their loss and not mine. That attitude is not a sense of arrogance but one of supreme self-confidence. I was to apply this lesson in years to come as it is as relevant to advisors dealing with their clients as it was to me dealing with my panel of advisors.

This has been a constant theme of my public speaking, where I encourage agents to profile their clients and only to deal with those that are worth dealing with. There is no need to chase everyone who might do business, just concentrate on those who value and appreciate what we do. This will allow us to mutually enjoy the relationship.

Consider for a moment, whatever business you are in your current attitude towards your clients and, in particular, your new prospects. Most people will answer that they seek to qualify to be their client's advisor (or other products or services provider). What about creating a perception of value that is so strong that we need our prospects to qualify to be our clients and customers? Is that not a better position to be in?

Considered individually, people attempt to place a value on one of either competency, professionalism or trust; delivered collectively, in an honest and caring way, competence, professionalism and trust are priceless commodities.

And this goes to the heart of *value creation*, the buzz phrase of success in the 2010s. In 2013, UK financial advisors have been profoundly affected by the regulator's Retail Distribution Review (RDR). This discussion of pricing for the right value has been the key concern of many advisors who seem to think that value creation is a quantifiable, empirical, almost magical numerical formula.

In my opinion, value creation is about creating the right emotional link with clients, such that they feel compelled to do business with us because of the joy and sense of freedom and trust we bring to the relationship.

That experience with my panel is still true today, where client relationships are key. During the global recession of around 2009 onwards, worried, concerned and frankly scared clients were looking for leadership from their key advisors. They needed to know that, as they went through a period of financial pain, we were there to support their decisions and to use our own entrepreneurial skills to help them through these difficult times.

Finally, this turbulent and challenging part of my life had taught me a further, very significant, lesson; that I needed to be in charge of my own destiny in order to be constantly ahead of change.

A Side-note on the Meaning of 'Value'

As I was writing this book, I happened to have a conversation with an accountant introducer about 'value'. I explained to him that I was increasingly finding that clients of accountants, who had previously been loyal and faithful were ditching their longstanding relationships with their accountants as they did not feel that they were receiving value.

He replied that he had never had anyone complain about his fees and disagreed with me.

I explained that, to these clients, value was not about price, but about how they feel their accountant was adding value as part of the relationship. Merely doing the accounts and filing their returns was no longer enough. Clients wanted their accountant to be thinking and behaving more pro-actively, identifying suitable opportunities for their clients to be more financially efficient, which was more than just tax planning (and most accountants I meet don't actually do creative tax planning other than moving some profit figures from one year to another).

They were more aware of opportunities through the media and colleagues and increasingly expected their accountants to be a source of access to these even if they didn't provide them themselves.

I continued my contention that accountants and lawyers have traditionally been reactive (as opposed to pro-active) professional advisors and were now vulnerable to commoditisation. That is, their basic services could be bought cheaply and conveniently and, in order to remain competitive, they had to find new and innovative ways in which to 'add value' to their client relationships. Reducing their hourly rate was not the point. They needed to work with other professions, particularly financial advisors, and those advisors also had to offer value-added services to what their competitors were doing.

Once we had discussed this in more detail, he appreciated the conversation and understood his vulnerability and appreciated the fairly simplified analysis.

Whatever your profession or career is, think about how you are genuinely and pro-actively adding value to your clients and customers.

The key question that you must constantly ask yourself is, *'what are you doing for your clients that they cannot do themselves?'*

This is the challenge for the 21st Century, where access to information and free advice is liberally available and people are increasingly accustomed to using the internet to source information in order to make their decisions. The problem with competing on price is that there will always be someone who will do it cheaper than you, even if it means making a loss, just to capture market share. Amazon is a good example of this.

As I was writing this book, several major businesses in the UK have simultaneously gone bust. Household names and established brands such as Comet (electrical), HMV (cds, DVDs and computer games), Jessops (cameras) and Blockbuster (DVD rental) no longer exist as major forces on the high street. The common theme between them all is that it was the internet and ready access to competitors that led to their downfall.

They failed to ask the question, *'what are we doing for our customers that they cannot do for themselves?'*

Successful people, whether they are in business or as employees wishing to further their career, need to work on their proposition to make it stand out from their peers and competitors. The detailed analysis of this is not the purpose of this particular book, and there are many other writers on this subject, and I intend to release a future book around this concept too.

In the meantime, be constantly aware of what is happening around you and the changes and trends that are coming, and always stay ahead of that change and be different. This is a theme I will continue to explore in this book.

11/ Swapping Teeth and the Challenge of Change

> *"Too many people go through life waiting for things to happen instead of making them happen."*
>
> *Sasha Azevedo, Actress*

I'd like to share an experience with you that, while being very amusing, has a profound moral to the story and helped to formulate many of my future decisions.

Some years ago, I was attending a family wedding in India. Over the course of the celebrations (Indian weddings have numerous functions over several weeks and are great fun!), many members of the extended family, covering several generations had gathered together and were staying in one house.

One evening, a few of my cousins had gone out for a few drinks and returned in a not too sober state. As they attempted to climb over the snoring bodies that were sleeping all over the house, they noticed that there were a large number of glasses of water beside some of the more elderly members of the family and floating like luminous jelly fish in these glasses were the false teeth of those deep in their slumber. With the bright moonlight reflecting off the pink and white dentures, this was indeed a surreal sight to behold. It was as if each tumbler was trying to talk, seeking release from the confines of its glass body.

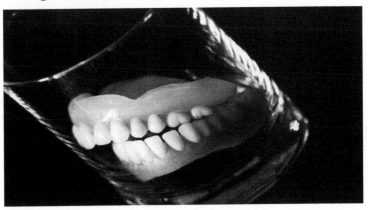

In an inspired moment of madness, my cousins decided to swap these teeth around the house, shifting and altering the glasses that accompanied each sleeper until even my cousins were totally confused as to whose teeth belonged to whom! They went to bed giggling and blissfully ignorant of the chaos that was to ensue in a few hours time.

Breakfast was very much a once in a lifetime experience! It was hilarious to see so many people struggling to chew their cornflakes and parathas[7] as their new, ill-fitting gnashers rattled loosely

---

[7] Indian flat bread, often stuffed, perhaps with potatoes

inside their mouths, their faces contorted in trying to secure them to their jaws!

At first, everyone was just too embarrassed to admit that something was wrong until, eventually one person who was really struggling asked if someone had mistakenly picked up his glass. That was when everyone else piped up about their discomfort. There then followed further surrealism as each of the toothless participants began a bizarre ritual of swapping their teeth with each other in order to regain some sense of normality. Whilst, for those having to undergo this ceremony it seemed traumatic, for those witnessing it, it had to be the funniest thing we had ever experienced!

Eventually, all were done in recovering their rightful chewing equipment except for one person. That individual was distressed to find that the teeth he had been left with were certainly not his. This was strange as, by definition, there could not be just one person with the wrong dentures, there had to be counterparty.

After further enquiry, it then turned out that another relative had found that his 'new' teeth were more desirable than his own and had kept quiet until it became obvious that he was the culprit!

So what's the moral of this incident? Firstly, it is a great example that change can be uncomfortable, as my relatives had found out with their teeth swapping episode. Secondly, and this is a profound point, change can lead to new, exciting and unexpected opportunities for the better, and this was about to become very apparent to me.

My career at Scottish Equitable was back on track and about a year after my unfortunate liaison with my warning letter, my relationships with my panel were so good, that I was effectively only working three days a week and I was comfortably and significantly ahead of my target while the company was well below its own target, which made me look even better. Life was good and I was enjoying lots of spare time. However, I was once again heading for a new Complacency Zone.

I woke up one morning and had a recollection of the swapping teeth episode and the insight that change can bring new and unexpected opportunities. I realised that I was starting to repeat the experience of a couple of years back, that I was sliding into a new Complacency Zone and that was not a pleasant time to wish to repeat. I came to a realisation that I needed to do something to change, the Comfort Zone was getting too comfortable again and I needed to do something radical. I also made an intuitive decision that I would rather put more effort into my career now, and take risks now in order to (hopefully!) enjoy an easier, more relaxed time later in life.

The career path at Scottish Equitable seemed to be something that would take too long. Furthermore, because of my performance, income was good and would have to reduce if I moved up the corporate ladder as it would mean giving up current bonus levels. If I was going to do that, then perhaps I should consider doing something else. I decided to leave the Comfort Zone and relative security of the corporate structure and became a self-employed financial advisor, selling to the public and fully in charge of my destiny.

Once again, I started to experience friends and relatives attempting to impose Glass Ceilings on me. I heard comments saying that I was taking too much of a risk, that I was giving up a good income, was I sure I knew what I was doing, that I had no client bank to support me, even that I was being foolish and reckless.

The biggest Glass Ceiling that was being forced upon me by other advisors was that I would be starting on the front line in January 1994, a significant date in UK financial services. There was a huge change about to happen to the profession because the UK financial services regulator had decided that the British public were somehow being misled by financial advisors, because they didn't know what the advisor was earning by way of commission on products that were sold. I thought that this was a pretty naïve way of thinking and the regulator's obsession with commission doesn't seem to have softened over the years as, in 2013, they decided to completely do away with commission payments for financial products. No other business required the vendor to disclose their profit on a sale, but it was the latest in a series of changes that were affecting the advisor community. In 1994, the regulator decided to introduce a system of commission disclosure which meant that whenever a product was sold, the client would have to be told in monetary terms, not percentages as previously, what the advisor was going to be paid by the product provider.

Many people were predicting this as the end of the profession on the grounds that, if the public knew what a financial advisor was earning, that people would not buy the products, or they would not continue to provide for the future or to protect their families. I was told I must be mad to want to become a financial advisor when everyone was terrified of the future. Why would I want to join a trade which was about to die out?

I thought long and hard about this and analysed the arguments. It seemed just like a Glass Ceiling to me. I could see how I could be successful and what I had to offer, but it was others who were trying to impose reasons that should prevent me. I considered what was likely to happen and concluded that, if anything, it would encourage the public to more greatly consider the value they were getting from their financial advisor. I don't necessarily just mean value for money, but what was the added value of working with a good advisor, as I defined earlier.

It would make people question what an advisor was doing for them to justify the income he/she was earning. Value was not something that could be quantified, but it was a feeling, an emotion of betterment, that an advisor could create with a client. A feeling that the client was moving ahead in their dreams and aspirations, that they had somehow created a greater sense of freedom and direction.

This was an interesting analysis as it was obvious to me from my experience of working with so many advisors that there were a large number that would find it difficult to justify what their added value was. It was not that they were bad or unethical advisors, it was just that they were keener to sell volumes of product rather than generate long-term relationships with their clients. As I declared earlier, I had learned lessons from those that were good at what they did and those that were not so good (I hesitate to call them bad). In my mind, I had a model of the kind of advisor I wanted to be.

It would be to do genuine, holistic, financial planning for clients and maintain unique, meaningful, valuable and enjoyable lifetime relationships, rather than simply selling a product and moving on. In fact, I could not understand how an advisor could be more focussed on selling his/her dreams and aspirations.

I felt that the clear transparency of commission disclosure would force advisors to change what they did for their clients and I fully recognised that change was a difficult thing to do. So, instead of this being a Glass Ceiling for me, I saw it as an opportunity. I did not need to change any bad habits or behaviour; I would be entering the role with no baggage, past experience or ingrained habits, but the opportunity to create a role for myself that had no preconceptions. The type of advisor I wanted to be was up to me to create.

I left Scottish Equitable and joined a firm on my panel, De Havilland Financial Management, as a pension specialist. It was a great company, with an emphasis on having fun while helping people and I had always enjoyed a great relationship with its owners, Cheri Gonsalves and Penny O'Nions.

As with most people who become financial advisors, who have to start from somewhere, I did the usual thing of phoning all the people I knew and offering my services. But very early on, I decided that I wasn't going to focus on selling particular products; most people would try to sell a savings plan or a pension or some life insurance. From day one, I would offer 'Holistic Financial Planning'.

I had noticed that some advisors had interpreted this as meaning that the goal was to sell all products to all and every client they saw. I had thought about it carefully and had come up with my own definition. I define Holistic Financial Planning as follows: How could I help a client to firstly recognise what it is that they want to achieve in their lives by helping them to think about their long-term plans and then by using my skill, expertise, knowledge and experience to find the solutions to help them to achieve these goals. These solutions *may* involve products that I could use and/or they may involve an introduction to someone with more specialist knowledge who could also help them. Perhaps a lawyer, accountant, stockbroker, trustee, actuary, etc. Sometimes, it might mean that I might not do business straight away, but that, by showing my clients that I genuinely cared about them, they would always come back to me when they were ready. I was building a business and enjoying relationships, not just pushing the latest products.

Understanding this, I wanted to quickly build up a database of professionals who could be part of my network. I started to attend every networking event going. I joined the London Chamber of Commerce and attended their weekly networking for business people events, and soon became a known face. There was almost a time when, if there was a networking event of some sort in Central London, there was a virtual certainty that I would be there.

At first, I would do what everyone does at these meetings, which was to gather as many business cards as I could in order to say that I had had a successful time. It was a like a boxing match to see who could get the most points, measured by the number of cards collected. I quickly realised that this was the wrong objective, and that the quality of the potential leads was far more important than the quantity of them.

Over the years, I have developed a great network of professionals that I can access on behalf of my clients. For example, when I meet business clients, as part of my fact-finding, it doesn't take me too long to identify that they often have other priorities that they need some help or support with. They may have a personnel issue, or marketing concern or a faster growth strategy that they are struggling to implement or perhaps need to work on an exit strategy; quite often, unless we establish these issues, they can easily be reasons for the client not to do business or take relevant action with us, as these matters are of greater concern to him. I explain that I could help them with these areas, but that they are not my prime areas of expertise and that they should meet our preferred firm of business coaches who can help them better than me. When I explain that once they have 'fixed' their problem, they will be in a better position to use my services, they respect that approach and are likely to be more loyal to what I offer them later.

I could see that Smashing this particular Glass Ceiling of establishing my own business identity and personal brand in the market place was going to be a fun challenge, but I needed a greater vision. I had already learned that it was dangerous to drift along and I needed to create a better sense of clarity of the future.

12/ Jigsaw Puzzles, the Pink Pound and the Media

> *"Be daring, be different, be impractical, be anything that will assert integrity of purpose and imaginative vision against the play-it-safers, the creatures of the commonplace, the slaves of the ordinary."*
>
> Cecil Beaton

Ask yourself the following question and give yourself thirty seconds to one minute to answer the question. I don't mean think about it for a minute before you answer the question, but immediately use the time to describe your answer in detail with whatever thoughts are in your head right now.

The question is, **'where do you see yourself in your personal and professional life five years from today?'**

Before you read on, you'll get much more value out of the comments that follow if you either talk to yourself aloud or write down your answer. Use as much description and detail as you can, but it should not require deep thinking or analysis. Simply, what is at the forefront of your mind?

Done?

Now, here are some thoughts to consider based upon the answer you gave yourself. If you had to pause before you answered the question, or if you said 'mmm', 'good question, let me think about it', 'maybe', 'possibly', 'if things go right', 'I'd like to...', 'maybe' or other similar vague, bland words and phrases, I'm going to put to you very bluntly that you don't yet have a Vision.

A Vision is something that is instilled in you, it is so clear to you and so important to you that it drives you forward constantly in order to realise that vision. If there is any vagueness in your Vision, then the achievement of it is likely to be equally vague. A high definition Vision of your own future is what gives you confidence and self-belief. The minute you use terminology that is fuzzy or lacking in clarity, you limit your own ambitions and sense of direction. Having a clear Vision is a very powerful tool for your success.

Let me put it to you another way with another question. Have you ever put together a 100 pieces, or 500 pieces or even 1,000 pieces jigsaw puzzle?

And, assuming that you did, did you do it without the picture on the box? Probably not, unless you really had nothing better to do!

And yet, if we can accept for a moment that a jigsaw puzzle is a good analogy for the journey of life, how many people will live their life *without* the picture on the box?

Think about when you get to the end of your life and, as you reflect on your achievements, you think about the picture you have created on the box of your life as a result of the pieces of life's jigsaw puzzle that you picked up along the way.

How would it feel if you then said that, actually given another chance, you recognise that there are some pieces you failed to pick up, there were some that you picked up a little too late and, indeed, some that you picked up that were never part of your puzzle anyway, but you held onto them because you thought they might be useful one day. Those pieces actually belonged to someone else, but you weren't prepared to let go, or delegate those things to someone else. Given another chance, you would have created a different picture by only picking up the right pieces and not wasting your time with irrelevancies.

Would it not be much better if you had a picture on the box of the next ten years (or more) that represented your Vision of the future? This picture would be in full colour, in full high-definition and it was now up to you to open the box and take out the pieces to make up your future life. A clear Vision gives you a template to know what pieces to take out in what order and what pieces to discard because they should not be part of your future; they're part of somebody else's puzzle but have inadvertently ended up in your box.

To continue the jigsaw puzzle analogy further, what is the first thing that most people do when constructing a puzzle? They usually put the corners down first. These are usually fairly easy to identify and, once they are correctly in place, they are immovable. Perhaps the corners represent our morals, ethics, beliefs and principles; they are non-negotiable.

And what usually happens next is that we look for the straight lines of the puzzle. This represents our future dreams and aspirations, our values and standards and gives the puzzle a clear edge and sense of scale. Within this framework, we can now identify the individual pieces we need to pick up to achieve our goals and objectives.

And, whenever, we are completing a puzzle, we don't just throw the pieces into the framework randomly, we tend to group natural areas together and work on several areas at the same time, building them up as we draw the connections together. A jigsaw puzzle is a great analogy for life.

Perhaps you now need to revisit your Vision statement and think about it again if it wasn't so clear first time around. Ideally, after several adaptations, you should get the statement to a condition where it drives you, guides you, motivates you and gives you a clear sense of direction.

The acid test will be if I were to ask you again **'where do you see yourself in your personal and professional life five years from today?'** and you simply cannot stop talking, with confidence, belief and conviction. There is no hesitation and the answer is on the tip of your tongue.

And here's my observation and experience of what happens with a sense of direction; not only does it drive you forward, it helps other people to recognise a sense of purpose with which you are living your life. And with that recognition, people want to be part of your life, they want to participate in your future if it is aligned with theirs and they want to help you achieve yours, as I was about to shortly find out.

During my role at Scottish Equitable, I had dealt with a very wide range of advisors, some with a clear vision and others who had no idea what was happening even the next day. One relationship in particular stood out with a financial advisor named 'Ivan Massow'. Over the years, Ivan has become a controversial character in financial services and more widely, with some strong opinions and alternative stances that frequently challenge convention.

I got to know Ivan when he ran a phenomenal financial advisory business in London, primarily because he had decide to focus on a particular niche market, the gay community. Being gay himself, he clearly understood his chosen market's needs and specific requirements. It was a niche sector that hit several significant key points. The sector is generally fairly affluent, with considerable disposable income (as a result of not having the usual costs of bringing up a family, for example) and willing to trust others to deal with their finances.

It was Ivan's focussed and disciplined approach to niche marketing that made a significant impact upon me. He would use various types of media to promote himself and his brand. He employed a PR agent, sponsored events such as the Gay Pride march and writing articles for his niche market's favoured newspapers and magazine. He branded himself as advisor to 'The Pink Pound' and became known as the 'go to' person for financial advice for the gay community. He positioned himself as the expert and did huge volumes of business, much of which helped me to hit my production targets. This knowledge of his secret to his business success would be very valuable and influential to me. It helped me recognise that, if I wanted to be a successful financial advisor, that perhaps I should also develop a niche market.

Almost on Day One as an advisor, I formulated a clear Vision, a picture on my jigsaw puzzle box of the future. My Vision was "to be recognised as the most professional advisor to the Asian community, at least in London, within five years". (In the UK we use the term 'Asian' to represent those from the Indian sub-continent as opposed to the Far East). The Asian community in the UK is very successful, fairly affluent and known for their entrepreneurial aptitude, so this was a sector that was worth targeting.

I should emphasise here that I was not suggesting that there were no other successful advisors to that community, but there were none who had achieved recognition of their expertise, no-one with a recognised reputation or brand.

You may have heard the phrase that 'a goal is a dream with a deadline'. Read my Vision statement above again and you will see that without the five year part, it was just a dream; the deadline converted the dream into a goal. Do your dreams have deadlines and timescales? If not, they will remain just dreams. Placing realistic timescales on your dreams creates a sense of urgency and movement. It makes you put a plan in to place to enable the dream to become reality.

Once again, I faced Glass Ceilings from those doubters who thought that business was too hard and that I was too far behind those that were already successful. I was told to find another niche or even not to have any niche and instead talk to anyone and everyone.

I could have taken notice of those Glass Ceilings and the negativity that pervades them...but I didn't. Instead, I placed my Vision as the picture on the box and now started to identify the pieces of the puzzle that I needed to pick up to bring my Vision into reality.

The first thing that I realised was that it was all very well for *me* to feel that I was the most professional, but I needed other people to believe it too. I had learned from Ivan that I needed the power of publicity to generate some name awareness, but I had no budget to pay for it

I surveyed the media that was focussed on the Asian marketplace and identified a weekly, English language, Asian newspaper, with a circulation of 40,000 per week called 'Eastern Eye' as being a candidate for my talents.

I requested a meeting with the newspaper's editor and proposed the idea of running a personal finance column to help educate the readership on financial matters. All the mainstream media were doing this and it seemed somewhat lacking for it not to be in Eastern Eye. I had prepared some sample articles to show the style in which I would write and a schedule of potential future articles. I also showed how the newspaper could then also target related companies for advertising, a sector that it currently ignored.

I explained that I did not require remuneration for this role, only that my name, photograph and contact details would be included in the strap-line. After some negotiation and introduction to the production team I would be working with, I was given the title of 'Finance and Business Editor' for Eastern Eye.

Under the heading of 'Money Matters', I started writing about the basics of financial planning, often using what was in the national weekend finance pages, but adapting it to my own style, and to suit the Eastern Eye readership. Crucially, there was never any hard sell or specific product promotion. My role was to educate and raise awareness, while raising my own public profile.

I was able to send the articles to prospects and create a library of articles in my office reception area, where new clients could read about my thoughts and opinions.

There is no denying that the media is a very powerful tool and so this was a chance for me to use that power to my own advantage whilst still providing a value added service to the community. It is incredible what the power of this form of third party endorsement can do. Whenever people see an author of an article, the automatic presumption is that you are indeed an authority on the subject, that you are somehow endowed with greater knowledge and expertise. Bearing in mind that I had only just become an advisor, this is quite a responsibility but it brings with it immense credibility.

For some articles, I also interviewed successful Asian business people to profile them as role models.

At parties and events, strangers would approach me and ask me if I was the person who wrote in the paper and compliment me on what I wrote. Over time, they would sometimes start asking if I could advise them and as my reputation developed, I would get phone calls from readers seeking personal advice.

Going back to my five-year Vision, my main objective of gaining recognition had been achieved, but now I needed to prove that I was one of the most professional advisors. It's great to have huge levels of self-belief, and this will certainly allow us to think bigger thoughts of what is achievable. But, there is a different sense of pride in being able to demonstrate that self-belief and self-confidence to your peers and the public. It reinforces and enhances that sense of confidence, prompting us to reach for even greater heights.

I was about to face yet another Glass Ceiling but Smashing it would be a life-changing experience and open even more doors...

13/ Too Young to Enter

> "If I have the belief that I can do it, I shall surely acquire the capacity to do it even if I may not have it at the beginning."
>
> *Mahatma Gandhi*

I want to share another story of what happens when you are prepared to confront the Glass Ceilings that are placed upon us. An example of what can happen if you never accept the word 'can't' but have the courage to say, 'let me show you how'.

A competition was announced by a trade magazine called 'Planned Savings' to find the best Independent Financial Advisor in the UK. This competition intrigued me as it seemed like an opportunity to discreetly test my own credibility. If I failed to win or even be shortlisted, no-one would know any better and...if I won (what an outrageous thought!)...if I won...it would bring me immediate status and recognition.

I had been an advisor for only one year and I made one of the most important decisions of my life and chose to enter the 'IFA of the Year' competition.

It seemed that whenever I made a profound decision, it would bring out the naysayers. Colleagues tried to place a Glass Ceiling on my ambition, saying that I was wasting my time, because I was not old enough or experienced enough. Some close friends even suggested that I should have learned my lesson from the Scottish Equitable interviews and that the judges would never award it to me because I was not 'blonde and blue-eyed', arguing that financial services in the mid-1990s was still a closed and narrow-minded place to be.

But rules are made for people who aren't willing to make up their own. I was not going to be deterred and decided to participate in the contest which was open to over 30,000 competitors.

The competition consists of writing a 2,000 word report in response to a case study question in one of 12 categories of financial services. I spent a considerable amount of time in preparing my report in the category of 'Retirement Planning for the Self-Employed'. I used some of the tools I had developed for client reports including the use of colour, tables, graphs and boxes to explain the advice. In 1995, this was cutting edge!

After submission of all the answers, the best three in each category are shortlisted and summoned to be interviewed by the panel of judges. To my pleasant surprise, I received an invitation, which meant that I had made it to the top 36 candidates. This was a daunting experience, as the panel throw you more questions and change some of the information to check your knowledge and adaptability.

I knew that this was not going to be easy. But I went there with a particular state of mind, deciding to use what others had said was a potential Glass Ceiling to my advantage. Others had said that my clearly visible identity, of which I am so proud, was a reason for those bigots that exist in the world to treat me differently. I hadn't realised that my absurd experience with John Wilkinson at the Scottish Equitable interview years earlier had actually left greater scars with some of my friends than it did with me.

I had no reason to believe that the panel of judges would behave less than honourably. In fact, I used my unique identity as an advantage. I took the view that, as long as I was at least as good as the other candidates, then it was my difference that would make the difference. That is, out of all the shortlisted 36 candidates, as long as I didn't make a fool of myself and was technically as competent as any of the others, I would be the one that the judges would remember afterwards. It is this philosophy of being different in order to stand out from the crowd that is a major theme of my life and a key message of this book,

A few weeks later, I attended the prestigious awards ceremony with 400 other advisors invited to witness the results. The author, Lord Jeffrey Archer was the guest of honour and host of the event.

The awards ceremony is just like the Oscars. The nominations for each category are listed one-by-one on the screen and the winner name is announced and asked to receive their award from the stage. After all 36 shortlisted names have been recognised, and 12 category winners announced, there is then the award for the overall 'IFA of the Year', the best of the best out of the 12 group winners. This is of course a very tense moment as none of the candidates knows any more than the fact that they are now in the top 36 and then in the top 12 for the overall award. Even as I am writing this, many years later, I still get goose bumps recollecting the experience.

Here's what Lord Archer said about the overall winner: "In the opinion of the judges, the IFA of the Year is highly motivated, highly qualified, with impressive technical expertise and excellent presentational skills". Sounds like a useful set of criteria to live one's life by whatever your career or profession.

Well, I'm very pleased to say that Lord Archer's description was about me and after winning my category, I also won the award for overall winner and was named 'IFA of the Year 1995'! When it was announced, I was overwhelmed and could not believe that it was my name that was being so enthusiastically applauded amidst the blaring music. It took me a few seconds to realise what had just happened before floating my way to the stage to receive the award. Peer group recognition has to be the best accolade that anyone can ever receive and this was one of the proudest moments of my life.

Eastern Eye was so overjoyed that their finance editor had won this prestigious national award, they put me on the front page of the next edition of the newspaper. It was a strange and surreal experience walking into my local newspaper shop and seeing my picture on the shelf!

But here's the biggest insight: my five-year goal had been achieved in just 14 months! It was astounding evidence that having a clear Vision accelerates time. Those without a Vision tend to drift along and then, five years later ask what happened. And they go further by saying, if they could relive it, they would do it a whole lot differently.

Compare that to those with a clear sense of their future destiny, who tend to achieve more than they can imagine and faster than they ever thought.

And here's another observation about having a clear Vision – amazing things will happen as a result of that Vision, amazing things that are well beyond our imagination. You see, having a clear and focussed Vision of our future instils self-confidence and self-belief; this confidence generates internal positive energy which manifests itself in our external posture (the way people see us). And, guess what? Just like us, those other people like to be around positive people – they want to share in our lives and to help us, as they feel that they too will somehow be energised from the experience of being part of our world.

For example, my raised profile put me in demand with various other publications, both Asian and mainstream, and soon I was re-producing articles that I had written for Eastern Eye into other forums.

In fact, with the level of self-confidence that I was sustaining, I was now charging publications for writing these pieces and gaining even greater profile.

Zee TV, a satellite TV channel, approached me and engaged me to present a series of TV programmes on personal finance. I was now able to convert my written skills into articulating them verbally and visually.

Off the back of this, I became something of a media personality, often being asked to demonstrate my experience on mainstream radio and television programmes, usually taking live phone calls answering people's questions about financial issues. I soon became a favourite for a number of channels as I understood that, in answering the viewers' questions, what was most important was to make it relevant to other viewers and listeners who may not have the same problem or question but could nevertheless learn from the discussion.

I was fast developing a skill to simplify complex matters and to avoid using jargon; in fact, recognising that members of the public need the jargon explained to them and would respect and appreciate someone who could do that for them, rather than someone who would show-off by using such confusing terminology.

Some of the skills I had learned as a student in

delivering speeches and presentations were now becoming very useful. I was invited to serve on various business committees, including as advisor to several government projects to encourage youth employment.

I was even asked to deliver a young entrepreneur's speech at the Bank of England, sharing some of the concepts that I have explained already in this book.

The point I am making by sharing these achievements with you is that positive energy is not something we switch on and off when we feel like it. It is something that we carry within ourselves (as my good friend Sol Hicks from Atlanta, Georgia puts it, "it is the light within us that we have to let shine") and its presence encourages other people to reach higher and attain new goals themselves.

As a result of Vision-inspired confidence, positive people constantly have an optimistic outlook on life and see opportunities which others pass by. They are driven by a sense of always having a destination and clear objectives. Their energy is inspirational.

By the way, here's a tip for you; if anyone around you is being particularly negative while you are trying to maintain a sense of positivity, simply call them an 'energy vampire' to their face. Explain that they are sucking the energy out of the situation and that if they have nothing positive to add, they should keep quiet!

Think about this for a moment: do you prefer to be around positive people or negative people? Positive, of course. And if that's how *you* feel, do you think other people might just think the same way? Absolutely they do.

I have said it before and I will repeat it: if they perceive us as being full of positive energy, generated from our clear sense of direction and purpose, incredible things will happen when other people feel compelled to join us for the ride. Allow me to share a phenomenal example of this with you in the next Chapter and to end this Chapter by explaining that winning the award opened up many opportunities. I was being courted by several companies to join them. However, I was fortunate enough to meet the incredible Caroline Banks, the winner of the IFA of the Year the year before me. For two years, we had a unique relationship as the only UK firm with two award winning financial advisors.

Caroline was the person who introduced me to the Million Dollar Round Table (MDRT) and little did we know back then that she would be the first non-American female President of MDRT in 2014; all of us in Britain are so proud of her!

In 1997, although very happy working with

Caroline, I decided that I wanted to run my own business and established my own financial advisory firm, Anand Associates, based in Central London.

And in 2003, I decided to Smash another Glass Ceiling, by entering the IFA of the Year competition once again. More Glass Ceilings went up as colleagues said that, out of a choice of 30,000 advisors, there was no way the judges would give it to the same person twice. By now, you'll know my answer to that!

This time I entered in the Protection category and after some more intensive judging by a panel, I was once again short-listed in my category. It was progress, but awards ceremony was unlikely to call out my name as a winner.

Once again, the audience went through the Oscars of the UK financial services profession and I am pleased to say that I was awarded winner of my Category...and winner of the overall title too!

I had Smashed another Glass Ceiling and was honoured to have

become the only advisor to have won this coveted award twice.

14/ Dinner with the Prime Minister

> *"Once you make a decision, the universe conspires to make it happen."*
>
> Ralph Waldo Emerson

I have already alluded to the value of having a clear sense of direction and the fact that other people want to be part of it. The following anecdote really brings home the value of this as things that are way beyond your imagination can occur if that sense of purpose is strong enough.

The Sunday Times newspaper in the UK publishes an annual listing of the Richest 1,000 people in the UK. This magazine supplement profiles these individuals and explains how they derived their wealth. In the course of compiling the Rich List, the researcher, Phillip Beresford, realised that he was seeing a large number of Asian names owning very successful businesses, many of them mainstream brands. Phillip approached the editor of Eastern Eye to offer him this list of the richest 200 Asians to publish as a magazine supplement with Eastern Eye, in a similar vein as the Sunday Times Rich List.

The editor accepted the opportunity and then had to source suitable sponsors to raise the funds to pay for the exercise. He looked for companies that would be suitably aligned to the high profile and prestige of this publication. With the profile for my company that I had been nurturing, the editor felt that Anand Associates would be a fitting partner as a firm already recognised as a creative provider of financial solutions to business owners.

This was a unique prospect and I was honoured to be selected as the first choice sponsor. My firm was only just over a year old and this would get us enhanced profile in exactly the right market place and generate even greater credibility. The decision was, however, not easy as it involved a cost that would exceed many financial advisors' marketing budgets that they may have allocated for ten years or more. Although difficult, it was too good an opportunity to miss, so I committed the funds and was appointed the lead sponsor of the publication.

By the way, I should mention in passing that the only other sponsor was a small, insignificant, firm some of you may have heard of called 'HSBC' bank![8]

I negotiated the sponsorship deal to include the database of the Top 200 and the centre four pages of the magazine. I also insisted on being seated next to whoever was going to be the guest of honour.

---

[8] In 1998, HSBC in the UK was known as 'Midland Bank'

Several months later, the launch event was booked and 400 distinguished guests were invited to the Café Royal hotel in Central London to a glamorous and prestigious dinner. This was to be the highest profile event of the Asian social calendar and I was right in the centre of it.

Earlier, I said that amazing things happen when we carry a clear sense of direction of our future and this was turning out to be an excellent example that other people want to play a part in our lives. What happened next, however, was way beyond any dreams or vision I had set myself. In fact, had I even dreamed of it and included it in my Vision, I would probably have been taken away by men in white coats and been locked up!

The Top 200 Richest Asians magazine launch party was graced by none other than the British Prime Minister, Tony Blair along with his wife Cherie, who came dressed in a traditional Indian sari. The event was all over the main TV news that evening and covered in all the mainstream press the next day. This was before the advent of Facebook, otherwise it would have gone global!

I had the honour of sitting next to Prime Minister Blair on the top table on stage for two and half hours, in front of the 400 prominent guests and, as lead sponsor, was Tony Blair's warm-up act delivering one of the most important speeches of my life. Mr Blair had only recently been appointed to the role of Prime Minister, after his landslide election in 1997 and (although things may have changed for him in later years), he was at that time extremely popular and gave a tremendous speech which acknowledged the value of Asian entrepreneurs to Britain's success. He was mobbed by the audience as he left and the event was a huge success. This kind of publicity and profile for my company was priceless and led to a number of those featured in the Rich List to become my clients.

The Glass Ceiling at the time was the cost of the sponsorship alongside whether this was the right thing to do for us at such an early stage of the business. There were, once more, some of the negative comments such as how could we possible compete with an organisation the size of HSBC?; almost from the perspective of how dare we even consider ourselves in the same league.

Had I taken notice of these comments and their limiting beliefs, then I would have saved a lot of money, but missed a massive opportunity. Instead, and as always, I took the attitude of 'let me show you why this is the right thing to do' and 'what is there stopping me competing with HSBC?'

Indeed, on the day, HSBC were not even noticed; they had no representation on the stage and no opportunity to speak and it was as if they did not

Prime Minister, Tony Blair, launches the Britain's Richest 200 Asians magazine at the Cafe Royal Hotel in London

exist.   As far as any attendees were concerned, Anand Associates was the only sponsor!

The message is that sometimes we need to have the courage to take risks, and that with a clear Vision to guide that courage, amazing things will happen that are way beyond that Vision.   Being willing to commit to the sponsorship was a huge risk at such an early stage of my business but with the courage and belief that it was the right thing to do, it created one of the most unique and memorable events of my career.

I hope that this episode serves as a good example of how Smashing the Glass Ceiling actually means challenging our own limitations of what is possible and never accepting the limitations that others might choose to place upon us.

Think of a project that you would like to do right now that just seems too big or too ambitious. Instead of concentrating on the reasons why you can't do something, write down all the benefits that would arise from achieving that goal.   What difference would it make to your life?

Now, in the context of what it means to you, and how it fits into your life's jigsaw puzzle vision, are you prepared to sacrifice something now (e.g. time, money, etc.) to achieve that?

14/ Revisiting your Glass Ceilings...and a Free Guarantee

> *"In the end, it's not going to matter how many breaths you took, but how many moments took your breath away"*
>
> *Shing Xiong*

This first book of mine has been a labour of love for me. I have shared some very personal stories and events that only a few people have previously known.

I have done so, not because I am anyone special or particularly talented or gifted. I'm not a mountaineer, an explorer or an athlete with amazing abilities. I've not had to overcome major disability or poverty or severe setbacks. I'm just an ordinary person who happens to have achieved some extraordinary things, through passion, belief and Vision and breaking a few significant Glass Ceilings along the way.

The real point is that, if I can do it, you too could do the same. I do not have any special skills or abilities, except perhaps an attitude of never being accepting 'no' as an answer. I hope to have shown that, by challenging the preconceptions of others and their limiting beliefs, amazing things can be achieved.

Remember, that success starts with first removing the barriers that keep us locked down, Smashing those Glass Ceilings that others impose on us.

Once we accept that we are surrounded by people who live their lives looking through their own Glass Ceiling of limitations (and we refuse to live by their rules), we then need a clarity of Vision to set meaningful and challenging goals, so that we see way beyond our self-imposed limitations. This Vision not only guides us but also motivates us.

And remember, that reaching a goal is not the end objective. Without further new challenges (maybe in different aspects of our life), a Confidence Zone will gradually become a Comfort Zone that gradually slides into a Complacency Zone; we must be constantly prepared to make strategic decisions to keep ahead of change.

Our self-confidence, along with our clear Vision, creates a sense of direction for us; we know what we continually want in life and know it is achievable so that we exude positive energy and self-belief. It is not something we switch on and off or choose to instigate by talking to ourselves in a mirror. It is our internal vitality and drive that others experience when they meet us. Some people call this your 'aura'; you know it when you meet someone and are intrigued by them, by the fact that they just have something different about them but you can't tell what.

You portray your positive aura when you carry yourself with pride and confidence in everything you do. Your drive passion and ambition are so unique and alluring that others want to be a part of what you are doing. You cannot switch your aura on and off, it is the essence of what you are and this force leads to amazing things.

What's your Vision for the next 5 years of your life? After reading this book and the instructions from one of the early chapters, can you now answer this question without any ambiguity or delay? If not, then please do go back and try the exercises again. If you are clear about it, then what if you stretched this Vision to ten years? Or more?

After reading this book, what will be your new, raised, Confidence Zone? Write it down and keep refining it until it is always in your mind. Turn up the colour of this Vision, make it widescreen and high definition and give it surround sound. Keep at it until you feel energised by it. You will notice the difference and I predict that extraordinary change will happen in your life.

But, before any of this, before you can move forward, you have to recognise what is currently holding you back and then address those issues.

What are the Glass Ceilings that are suppressing you; are they being imposed on you or are they really self-imposed limited beliefs? I hope that I have shown you that all of these Glass Ceilings can be Smashed by changing your attitude towards them.

Here's a further example of what I mean by *attitude*: Two people walk into a room full of strangers. Person A thinks, 'Oh my God, I don't know anyone here. What am I going to do? This is going to be so boring; I'm going to just stand in the corner and hope that no-one tries to talk to me; I hope it finishes soon; I can't wait to get out!'

Person B thinks, 'Oh my God, I don't know anyone here. This is going to be so exciting; I wonder who I might meet that could be really fascinating; I wonder what opportunities may arise when I share some stories; this is going to be fun; I hope I have enough time to see everyone!'

Be honest with yourself, are you Person A or Person B?

Person A is living that moment under a Glass Ceiling whereas Person B Smashed his Glass Ceiling before he entered the room. The same circumstances and the same opportunities, but the difference in *attitude* is what will determine the

168

results.

Never, ever, let there be a barrier to your dreams, apply the transforming power of looking for the opportunity in each and every situation and destroy those Glass Ceilings!

Remember, before we can set the world alight, we have to be on fire ourselves!

So, join me in Smashing your personal Glass Ceilings, to liberate your dreams and aspirations to the sunshine and blue sky of success beyond!

Having shared my experiences with you and various strategies that you could implement into your thinking that could change your mindset, I hope that you now feel that a lot more confident and full of self-belief.

Are you ready to *finally* Smash those Glass Ceilings that you wrote down earlier in the book?

Take out the exercise you did earlier of writing out a list of your current Glass Ceilings. Remember, we had already changed the perspective on this list by changing the heading of it from **'My Glass Ceilings'** to **'My Opportunities'**, vividly illustrating that the discussion is really about our *attitude* towards things; if we view them as obstacles, then they are. And, if we view them as opportunities, this book has shared some of the amazing things that can happen.

Now, look at that list once again. Knowing what you know now and recognising the need to remove the word 'can't' from your vocabulary, how do you now view that list?

Try this: change the heading on your list once more; cross out **'My Opportunities'** and change the title to two new words **'My Excuses'**.

Consider those words at the top of your list for a few moments. Do you now agree that what you initially perceived as your Glass Ceilings are really just Excuses; I put it to you that they are largely in your head and they are a choice you make.

So, what's going to be the first step you take now to implement change?

I know from my speeches all around the world that my ideas have worked for people. Many, many people have told me that their lives have been changed by implementing just a few of the concepts that I shared in this book; and there will be many more in forthcoming books. The question is: 'will you be one of them?'

As I have already explained and demonstrated – it's up to you!

Oh, and my guarantee? Very simple. I guarantee

that if you do not use an idea, it is guaranteed not to work!

I look forward to hearing about your phenomenal success.

15/ Epilogue - Inspire a Generation

I constructed and wrote this book over the course of 2012 and early 2013. I was reminded several times that, according to the Mayan Prophecy, the world was predicted to end in the latter part of 2012 and that there was little point in writing a book for which no one will be around to read! Sounds like a Glass Ceiling to me.

More importantly, 2012 was an extremely important year for Britain as we were honoured with hosting the London Olympic Games which, beyond all possible expectations, were supremely magnificent. London was show-cased as undeniably the greatest city in the world and I was proud that it was my hometown. The Capital was buzzing with energy and vibrancy and the world came to visit.

My office is in Central London and it was sheer joy to witness the various nationalities parading past my window on a daily basis during that glorious summer of sport.

It was interesting to note how some of people suffering from the Glass Ceiling syndrome had chosen to flee London for Fear of the transport system Failing or even the Fear of a terrorist attack. Instead, many people, who preferred the feeling of a Desire for Success for the Games, were rewarded with an electric and genuinely once in a lifetime experience.

Getting tickets for any of the Games' events was not easy but I managed to see several events including joining 50,000 ecstatic people in Hyde Park watching the athlete, Mo Farah, win the 5,000 km race to gain his second gold medal of the Games. It was an incredible, memorable and totally unique occasion.

I also managed to get tickets to the Paralympics at the Olympic Stadium and it is undoubtedly a testament to Britain's tolerant society that these events were as well attended and supported as the main Games – my, how things have moved on since my tangle with John Wilkinson and his bigoted views!

It was awe-inspiring to see disabled athletes taking part in sport at a level at which even able-bodies people would be frozen with Fear. It was jaw-dropping to see blind runners running down the track led by their sighted guides with whom they shared a handcuff of faith.

The most amazing for me were the blind triple jumpers. The athlete would be led carefully by his guide to his starting point on the run-up and be precisely pointed to face the right direction. His guide would then go down the track and stand by the sand pit and the audience would become completely silent. From there, he would then guide the athlete down the track as the athlete would hurtle at top speed towards his destination, his guide shouting at him to move left or right and then, finally, just at the right, crucially vital, moment, when to start his steps and leaping, launching himself into the soft and welcoming sand.

On some occasions, the athlete would veer slightly off the correct direction and their guide would stop them and start again. On some run-ups, however, the athlete would not be able to stop in time and would run directly into the judging official, innocently sitting by the leaping board, both of them tumbling and entangled with the chair. I was pleasantly surprised there were no serious injuries.

I was struck by the utter bravery and courage of these completely blind athletes. For them, the fact that they could not see was not a Glass Ceiling. What was abundantly clear was the fact that although the athletes had no sight did not mean that they had no Vision. In their mind, they could see spot from where to jump, they had visualised the fine grains of sand giving them a soft landing, they could feel the glory of standing at the top of the medals podium and the emotion of hearing their national anthem. It was obvious that their Desire for Success far outweighed their Fear of Failure.

It was this visible positive attitude, determination and confidence that they possessed that made their guides want to work with them. It was their sheer blind faith in their future success that made these athletes want to fully exploit the potential that they had. They had no barriers, no obstacles and they certainly had no Glass Ceilings left to destroy.

Perhaps it was just fate or simple co-incidence that this book was written in an Olympic year, with so many amazing sporting analogies that could be applied to the process I have described in this book.

I stated several times that I am not a special individual, I don't have any particular talent or artistic flair, I haven't climbed a mountain or faced death and survived and I don't have any disabilities that needed to be overcome. And I certainly do not compare my humble achievements to any of those people that have overcome such massive hurdles.

I cannot, and do not, compare myself to these incredible athletes, but I am inspired by their stories and events such as the London Olympics. I am constantly motivated by examples of where people have Smashed the Glass Ceilings that were placed there either by others or their own lack of self-belief.

In sharing how I have Smashed some of my personal Glass Ceilings, I hope that this book will encourage you to walk with a renewed sense of pride and confidence and faith that you too can obtain the gold medals you set out to gain and realise the Vision you have created.

I am aware of many people who have heard my 'Smashing the Glass Ceiling' speech and implemented the concepts and then gone on to achieve huge success in their lives and I look forward to hearing about your success and breakthroughs.

Take a few moments to consider what aspects of

this book you can learn from and adapt to your own personal circumstances.

What is your game plan for the next ten years, the next five years, the next 12 months and the next quarter.

What's the very first thing you need to do now?

When are you going to implement that?

Who is going to be involved with you to do that?

Reading a book like this is only the start of the process of change. And, as I explained earlier in an early chapter, this book is not going to give you the potential to succeed – you already have that within you. All I am attempting to do is inspire you with some stories that you can adapt to your own personal benefit.

Please do share with me your personal feedback via bhupinder@advisormasterclass.com and tell me about the Glass Ceilings you have Smashed!

Good luck, aim high, think big and have fun!

16/ Financial Advisor Master Class

> *"The significant problems that we face cannot be solved at the same level of thinking we were at when we created them"*
>
> Einstein

What is it that clients *really* want from a financial advisor?

Is it a set of products or is it a trusted relationship?

Whichever it is, it's essential not just to be the best there is, but to offer something *different* to the competition.

Einstein shares a thought with Bhupinder!

Advisors that recognise and understand their valued role in financial planning, allied to appreciating the needs of their target market, are able to command higher rewards by offering a tailor-made solution and long-term relationship. And they have incredible fun along the way, with greater satisfaction of having made a difference to their clients and the other people around them.

The Advisor Master Class™ and Advanced Advisor Master Class™ are programs designed to help financial advisors transition from being sales agents to becoming trusted, holistic, financial planners.

Through his whole-day programs, Bhupinder Anand shares his proven ideas, practical techniques, personal experiences and transferable strategies for success.

Indeed, many delegates have reported that they have recovered the Master Class fee on their first client using their newly- learned techniques. Many have also hit new record levels of production, reaching their Elite Club, etc., within just a few weeks of attending a Master Class.

The Advisor Master Class was formed when Bhupinder realised that there was so much more he could share than was ever possible in a one hour keynote or focus session speech and, actually, through demand from conference attendees wanting more detail.

It has now been held in many countries and many delegates have attended several times, learning more things each time.

If you would like to attend a future Advisor Master Class, please visit www.advisormasterclass.com and register your interest.

If you would like to organise an Advisor Master Class for your group or company, then please do make contact with Bhupinder by email at Bhupinder@advisormasterclass.com or phone +44 207 486 5486.

If you would like to order more copies of this book for your friends, company or association, please contact enquiries@advisormasterclass.com or phone +44 207 486 5486.

Or, just email the above address to be added to our database to be kept informed of future books and other relevant material or courses.